Get Going With AVR

Errata Sheet

This book is a few years' old and events have moved on in the software and microcontroller worlds since it was written. However, basics like numbering systems, programming principles and electronic design have stayed the same, so the vast majority of this book is as relevant today as when it was written.

The descriptions of the AVR range, the development tools available and the instruction set, Interrupt Vectors and Memory Map are out of date.

P38 – AVR Range.

This range has now expanded greatly and the AT90S devices have been replaced by ATtiny and ATmega AVR parts. This book refers to the 20 pin AT90S1200 and AT90S2313 and the 40 pin AT90S8515 for most of its examples. The AT90S1200 has no direct replacement, as it has a hardware stack and no onboard SRAM. But the AT90S2313 is equivalent to the ATtiny2313 and the AT90S8515 is the same as an ATmega8515

P88 – Development Systems

The de facto development system for the AVR is now Atmel's AVR Studio 4, which is far and away the best microcontroller development environment available. Kanda AVR ISP, STK200 AVR board and AVR JTAG ICE are ideal for use with AVR Studio and form a comprehensive development environment. AVR Studio 4 and a guide to using it are included in the CD supplied with the book.

Appendix B

The memory map of newer AVR devices is much larger although it follows the same format. See any AVR device datasheet for a more complete list of the special function registers at the bottom of FLASH. A few extra instructions have been added for recent AVR microcontrollers e.g. SPM – Store Program Memory.

Interrupts

Newer AVR devices also have more interrupts and the Interrupt Vector Table that is placed at the beginning of your program if interrupts are required will also be different. Again, see the datasheet for the device you are using.

GET GOING WITH . . . AVR MICROCONTROLLERS

AN INTRODUCTION TO

AVR

MICROCONTROLLERS

REVISION 1.0

PETER J SHARPE

GET GOING WITH ... AVR MICROCONTROLLERS

The information contained in this publication has been prepared in good faith using information currently available.
No liablility is assumed by Kanda Systems, Atmel, IAR, or the author for the accuracy or use of the information, or infringement of patents arising from such use.

Copyright Kanda Systems Ltd 1997. All rights reserved. Except as permitted under the Copyright Act of 1976, no part of this publication may be reproduced or distributed in any form or by any means, or stored in a database or retrieval systems, without the prior written permission of Kanda Systems Ltd.

The Atmel logo and name, AVR and STUDIO are registered trade marks of Atmel Corporation in the USA.
The Kanda logo and name are trademarks of Kanda Systems in the UK.

ISBN 1 902179 005

Copyright Kanda Systems Ltd

Kanda Books, Unit 17, Glanyrafon Enterprise Park, Aberystwyth, SY23 9PQ

First published 1997

CONTENTS

PREFACE v

1 INTRODUCTION
Introduction to microcontrollers. 1
The need for a new approach 3
The AVR concept 5

2 MICROELECTRONIC SYSTEMS 7
Electrical signals 7
Logic 12
Micro-based Systems 18
Number systems and manipulation 30

3 AVR MICROCONTROLLERS 37
Range and Functions 38
Circuit requirements (Clock /Reset) 41
Programming Model 47
Instruction Sets and Addressing Modes 53
Input/Output 65
The Stack, Subroutines and Interrupts 70
Special Functions 75

4 PROGRAMMING THE AVR 84
Planning your programmes 84
Development Systems 88
Programming the AVR 91
Example applications 92

GET GOING WITH . . . AVR MICROCONTROLLERS

5	**CLEVER STUFF**	114
	Accessing Look-up tables	114
	Using EEPROM	117
	Assembler Update	121
	Analog applications	122
	Timers and Counters	
	PWM methods	
	Using the watch dog timer	134
6	**POTENTIAL CLEVER STUFF**	137
	In-Circuit Emulation	137
	Programming in C	138

APPENDICES
GLOSSARY OF TERMS	A
INSTRUCTION SETS	B
REFERENCES	C

INDEX

GET GOING WITH ... AVR MICROCONTROLLERS

PREFACE

Welcome to the exciting world of embedded control and the incredible AVR microcontroller. Thank you for buying, receiving or otherwise acquiring this book. I hope you find it useful.

The AVR is a new product range and at the time of writing was hot off the silicon press (my development work was done on mostly early-production samples and Beta release software!) Please be aware of this when designing hardware/firmware with the aid of this book, things may have changed! Technical details are subject to change without notice, it pays to check the latest technical data from Atmel. (I need some excuse for any errors you find!)

I have structured this book in an attempt to fulfil the needs of enthusiasts, design engineers, students, and those poor misguided souls (like myself) who struggle to teach microelectronic systems in an underfunded further education environment. I hope I have succeeded.

I wish to thank all those people who helped in Atmel, IAR, Chippenham College, and especially Kevin Kirk and Adrian Wallis of Kanda Systems for their support and providing the opportunity to write this book. This book is dedicated to my students, who acted as guinea pigs (and still are!) and to my wife Janette, daughter Lucy and son Ben, in an attempt to make up for hours sat in front of a computer!

Peter J Sharpe

GET GOING WITH . . . AVR MICROCONTROLLERS

1 INTRODUCTION

INTRODUCTION TO MICROCONTROLLERS

The impact of the microprocessor on the modern world is well known, computers, cash machines, the world-wide web, are just a few examples. What may not be so widely understood is the quiet revolution occurring within our normal everyday objects which we take for granted. Items like washing machines and other household appliances, telephones (mobile or otherwise), cars, and even toys (have you bought a Cyberpet yet?), can now contain microcontrollers of some form. The modern world demands cheap and simple to use products which do a lot. Simple control of complex items requires processing power.

Microprocessor based systems (as used in computers) are not cheap, even at 8-bit level, requiring expensive support chips, relatively large printed circuit board area (even with SMT) and expensive program development equipment and time. The fairly recent invention of the microcontroller has changed this for ever.

A microcontroller is a single chip containing all the circuits required to make a computer for control applications.

GET GOING WITH ... AVR MICROCONTROLLERS

These are then mass produced bringing the price down to a few pounds (dollars, euro etc.) per device. They have been widely used in industrial and domestic equipment for some years, mainly in 4-bit or 8-bit form. (**ALL** VCRs, most modern TVs and many cars have at least one!) Complex programming and specialist (expensive) development equipment have kept these in the domain of the specialist, cost and complexity precluding their use by most enthusiasts or very small businesses. The widespread use of them in other areas only started when Arizona Microchip launched a simple to use range of microcontrollers called the **PIC**. (**P**rogrammable **I**nterface **C**ontroller). Suddenly microcontrollers became accessible to everyone because they were so cheap to buy, and relatively easy to use and program.

The decision whether to use a microcontroller or conventional electronics is usually made on the basis of cost and/or facilities. Conventional logic gates and other electronic building blocks, such as operational amplifiers, are cheap, but they do need a lot of printed circuit board space and are limited in what they do.
With the advent of cheap microcontrollers the decision is made for you. Most applications requiring more than a few chips can be made cheaper, smaller, and provide more functions, using microcontrollers. This is changing the face of electronics rapidly. Those of you who have made circuits, breadboarded them, placed them on stripboard or printed circuit board, will know the time and effort involved in laying out the board and getting the circuits working, With microcontrollers the time and effort is largely transferred to getting the program working, the hardware being a minor job! The performance of the finished product is now only limited by your imagination.

GET GOING WITH ... AVR MICROCONTROLLERS

THE NEED FOR A NEW APPROACH

The problem with most microcontrollers is the time taken to develop the programmes. The usual process is :-

1. *Buy an expensive EPROM version (£20 or so)*
2. *Develop the program in assembly language on a PC*
3. *Simulate it on the PC and debug it until it works!*
4. *Blow the EPROM version and place in the target board*
5. *Tear your hair out when it does not work!*
6. *Repeat the process from step 2 until it works*
7. *Blow your program into a cheaper (£2 or so) One Time Programmable (OTP) version for the finished product.*
8. *Test it, and throw it away if it does not work (OTP means ONCE ONLY)!*
9. *Relax and wait for the money to roll in.*

If you are lucky, or have plenty of money, or both, you may have an **I**n **C**ircuit **E**mulator (ICE) which pretends to be your microcontroller but is attached to the PC. This saves a lot of development time and means that you can be fairly confident that your program will run before you program the microcontroller.

The development of the program is a major task with some microcontrollers. Some have huge instruction sets and are very slow to execute programmes (CISC types usually), others are very fast (RISC usually) but have a very limited instruction set.

GET GOING WITH . . . AVR MICROCONTROLLERS

Programming in assembly language is also an acquired skill which does not suit everybody! It would be nice to be able program in a high level language if you wished and have both fast program execution and a rich instruction set to choose from.

Most microcontrollers can be programmed in high or medium level languages, `C' for instance. The code produced by the compiler is usually not very compact because it is difficult for the compiler to match high level statements with the machine code of the microcontroller. (Microcontrollers do not have `buckets' of memory to play with like PCs). The speed of execution is also that much slower because of the larger code. You might even have to buy a larger, more expensive microcontroller to get more memory because of this!

Some applications demand fast `number crunching' and signal processing, as well as control. Data telemetry is one such example (Remote Control and Monitoring). Most 8-bit systems are incapable of this at any respectable speed which usually means employing a 16 or 32 - bit processor based system and these are expensive!

It would also be nice to be able to update the program repeatedly in the microcontroller WITHOUT, high voltage (12v) supplies, expensive EPROM versions or special programmers, and in-circuit if needed. This would reduce the need for an expensive ICE system.

You now have some inkling of the AVR concept.

GET GOING WITH ... AVR MICROCONTROLLERS

THE AVR CONCEPT

It occurred to the Norwegian members of the Atmel design team (some of whose initials make up AVR!) that a new approach was needed. They went to work and came up with :-

- *The latest and fastest low power 8-bit HCMOS RISC technology was used in the design to produce a very fast beast, capable of out performing larger 16 bit processors and exceeding the speed of standard CMOS logic! (Sixteen Million Instructions Per Second (16 MIPS) is easily attainable giving 62.5 ns per instruction!)*

- *`C' is the most popular and efficient programming language at present (C++ on larger micros) so the AVR instruction set was actually designed around the `C' compiler. Code conversion is thus very efficient and fast. You can still program in assembly language if you wish, but at least you now have a sensible choice!*

- *FLASH programming technology, combined with a fast Serial Peripheral Interface (SPI) enables repeated erasing and downloading of the program with the same power supply as the circuit, AND in circuit if necessary via a simple link with the PC! This allows the operating system of your design to be changed from outside and even remotely via the World Wide Web! The microcontroller is also the same (CHEAP) one that you will use in production. No special EPROM or OTP versions are required.*

What you gain with FLASH technology

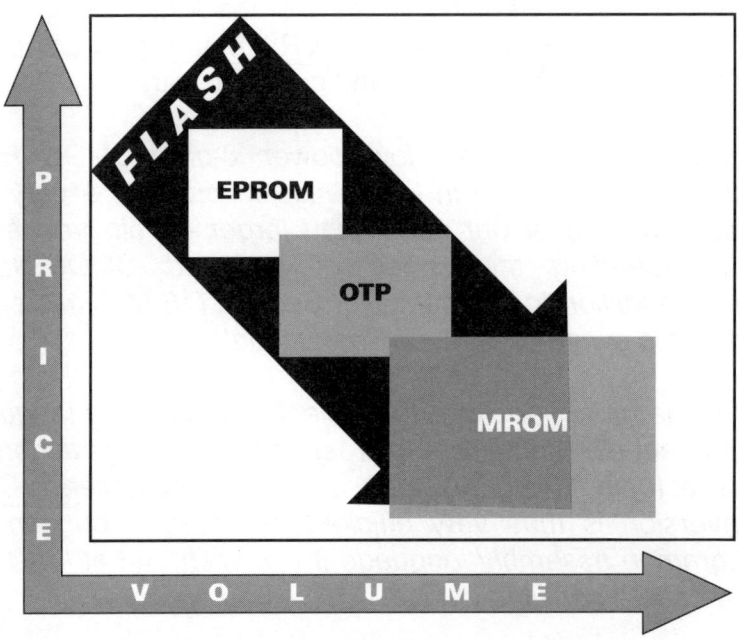

(Diagram: Courtesy of Atmel Corporation.)

One AVR FLASH device, instead of three possible other types, EPROM for development, OTP for small production quantities and MROM for mass production quantities.

The end result is a very cheap, fast and easy to use range of microcontrollers which is likely to wipe the floor with the competition!

2 MICROELECTRONIC SYSTEMS

This chapter covers basic electronic theory concerning signal processing and assumes little prior knowledge. You can safely skip this chapter if you are already familiar with digital logic, microprocessors and number systems.

ELECTRICAL SIGNALS

Microelectronic systems are those systems using microelectronic components, usually **I**ntegrated **C**ircuits (ICs). Since this accounts for virtually all modern electronic equipment the definition has evolved to mean those systems employing a **M**icro**P**rocessor **U**nit (MPU or micro.,).

The job of all electronic systems is to process electrical signals. These signals can be in one of two forms, ANALOGUE or DIGITAL. Micros are digital systems but can be made to process both types, although the conversion from one type to another can be a real pain and far from perfect. Human beings, and mother nature, produce and respond to signals which are analogue in nature. *We are instantly in conflict with nature!*
It would be easier to use an analogue system of course, but this is not convenient, as we shall see. The main problem with analogue systems is electrical noise (unwanted signals) generated either by the components themselves or picked up from outside sources (interference).

GET GOING WITH . . . AVR MICROCONTROLLERS

ANALOGUE SIGNALS - vary continuously with time, normally between voltage levels of two set limits (the supply rails usually), and are used to represent some external measurement (audio, video, temperature, fluid level etc.,) They can thus be carried over two wires, the signal wire and the ground return. This is the form of most signals derived from real world situations via suitable TRANSDUCERs (e.g. microphone, guitar pick-up, temperature probe).

TYPICAL ANALOGUE SIGNAL WAVEFORMS

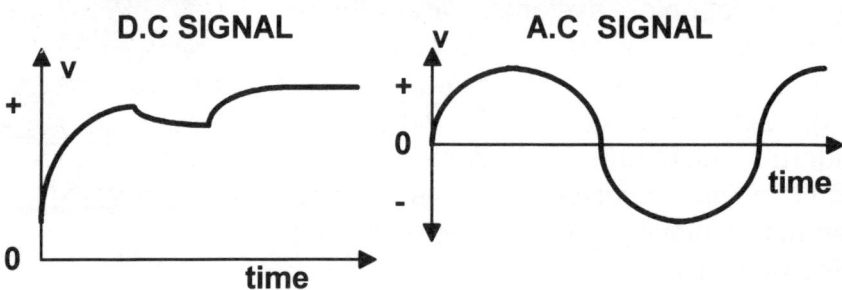

Note that the DC analogue signal varies from one level to another but is always equal to or greater than the 0v supply rail. This is typical of the signals obtained from temperature sensors and fluid level detectors, and represents a change of level. (It is also the shape of a DC supply such as a battery).

The AC analogue signal varies SINUSOIDALLY above and below 0v (alternates positive and negative) and is the type of signal derived from audio transducers, such as microphones. (It is also the shape of the AC mains voltage supply).
It contains amplitude (Volume) and frequency (Tone) information.

GET GOING WITH . . . AVR MICROCONTROLLERS

DIGITAL SIGNALS - vary discontinuously with time (jump in steps), normally between two set levels (the supply again). The usual digital signal consists of TWO levels and is hence called a BINARY (BI=2) digital signal having a logic ZERO (usually near 0v) and a logic ONE (usually near the positive supply rail e.g. +5v). Since the signal can only represent two levels, off and on, it carries a very limited amount of information. It is, however, ideal for transistors, which work best as solid-state switches.

TYPICAL DIGITAL SIGNAL WAVEFORMS

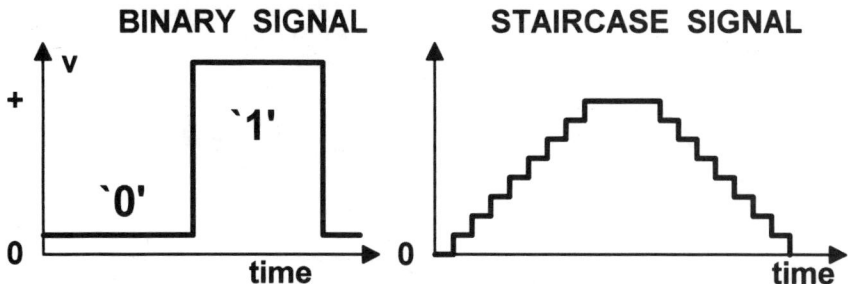

The binary signal is the type processed by micros and logic gates and the one most commonly recognised as digital. The logic level represents one **BIT** (derived from **BI**nary digi**T**) of information carried on one wire (plus a 0v return of course).

The staircase waveform is technically a digital waveform since it has discontinuities (steps). It is more often taken to be an analogue signal obtained as a result of a Digital to Analogue Conversion (DAC) and should be a smooth curve or line (the steps should not be there)! This is the result of low resolution conversion in the hardware and can be improved by taking more bits in parallel over several wires to reduce the size of the step. The signal can then be filtered to smooth out these small steps.

GET GOING WITH ... AVR MICROCONTROLLERS

You may well ask why digital has become so popular if it involves so much more wiring! The answer is mainly improved noise performance, ease of processing (Analogue processing is a nightmare) and good availability of processing devices. Analogue computers do exist, but they are difficult to program and inaccurate. Digital computers are cheap and freely available in many forms. They can also be made very accurate by using larger parallel WORD sizes.

NOISE IMMUNITY IN SYSTEMS

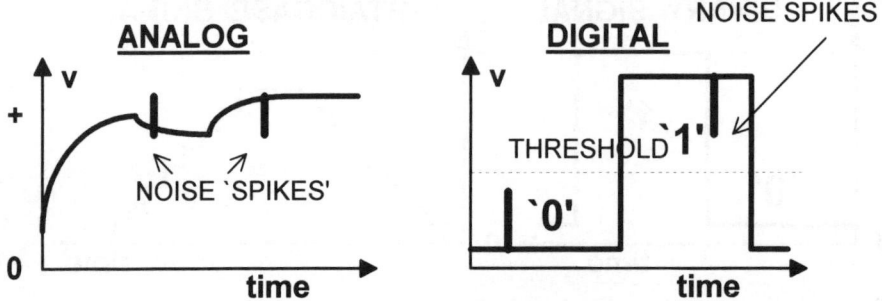

Electrical noise commonly appears as interference `spikes' on the signal. On the analogue signal nothing can be done to filter this noise `spike' apart from suppress the source of the noise.

On a binary digital signal the system looks for a set threshold level to be exceeded before it decides if the value is a `0' or a `1'. The noise spikes would have to be large enough to push the level past the threshold to cause an error. Noise of this magnitude is rare thankfully, making digital systems very much more reliable than analogue versions. (Hence CD players, digital NICAM stereo, and now digital TV on the horizon!)

GET GOING WITH ... AVR MICROCONTROLLERS

The binary signal still carries frequency information but only two amplitude levels, `0' or `1'. The amount of information carried by a digital signal is thus very much smaller than analogue.
To achieve a similar quantity of information movement, many bits will be needed in parallel, involving many wires instead of just two (ONE for each bit plus a ground return). The number of bits used in a system for data is called the **WORD** size. It is rare to find single bit micros, but they do exist!

The number range which can be handled by binary digital signals is set by TWO to the power of the number of bits. In mathematical terms, **range = 2^n** where n is the number of bits employed. The table below gives the number ranges and resolutions (roughly the step size as % of power supply) for typical word sizes:-

WORD SIZE	COMMON NAME	NUMBER RANGE	RESOLUTION %
1	BIT	0 - 1	100
4	NIBBLE	0 - 15	6.25
8	BYTE	0 - 255	0.39
16	WORD	0 - 65,535	1.5×10^{-3}
32	DOUBLE WORD	0 - 4,294,967,295	2.33×10^{-8}
64	-	$0 - 1.844674406 \times 10^{19}$	5.42×10^{-18}

As can be seen 8-bit micros are plenty accurate enough for most control work if you can get the speed of processing fast enough.
32 or 64-bit micros are used in computers for fast data processing and graphical manipulation.

GET GOING WITH ... AVR MICROCONTROLLERS

The table also defined a few terms which are commonly used relating to word sizes. Bit is one bit, a nibble is four bits (half a byte), a byte is eight bits and then it gets confusing! Word is commonly used to mean a 16-bit word size, with 32-bits called a double word, but usage varies so beware, it is also used to describe the width of data used, giving 8, 16, or 32-bit word sizes typically!

LOGIC

N ow we can investigate how micros can process signals. The binary digital signal is processed by one of a few simple logic operators. These are AND, OR, NOT and EOR (or XOR). From these simple functions all other processes can be derived, including add, subtract, multiply and divide. It is important that we understand the basic logic functions before we attempt to use microcontrollers. The theory also introduces diagram symbols for logic gates and truth tables to display binary input/output possibilities. These are worthwhile persevering with as they make life a lot easier.

ANSI STANDARD LOGIC SYMBOLS

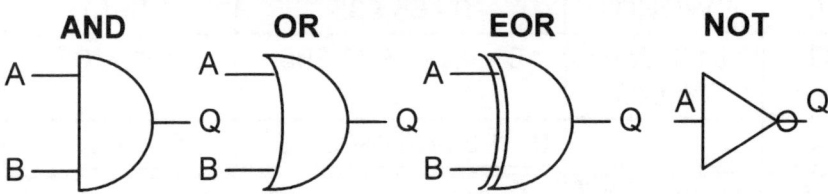

(Note, various logic symbols abound, ANSI (American), IEC (European) and BS (British Standard). The ANSI (MIL) spec., is the most popular, so we shall use these in all our diagrams.)

The AND function.

The AND function only gives a logic `1' out if all inputs are a logic`1'. All other possibilities give a logic`0' out. AND gates are available in IC form, usually more than one on a chip. The usual diagram symbol for the AND gate is shown below, along with the input output possibilities displayed in a TRUTH TABLE.

INPUT A	INPUT B	OUTPUT Q
0	0	0
0	1	0
1	0	0
1	1	1

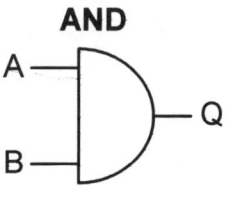

Note, that only two inputs are shown, A and B. There can be many more, with chips freely available with two, three, four or eight inputs. The principle remains the same, regardless of the number of inputs, just the truth table gets longer!

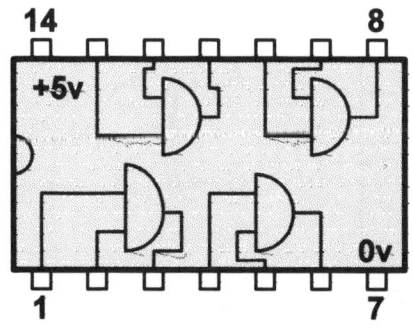

PINOUTS OF
QUAD TWO INPUT
AND GATE IN
HCMOS FAMILY

74HC08

The OR function.

The OR function gives a logic `1' output when any, or all the inputs are a `1'. (Sometimes called the `inclusive OR' because it includes the possibility when all inputs are `1'). The alternative way of looking at this is to say the output is only `0' when all inputs are `0'!

INPUT A	INPUT B	OUTPUT Q
0	0	0
0	1	1
1	0	1
1	1	1

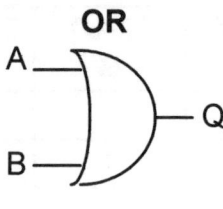

The EOR function.

The EOR (or XOR) is the exclusive OR function because it excludes the case when both inputs are a `1'. This gate gives a logic `1' output when any TWO inputs are different. The alternative way of looking at this is to say the output is only `0' when all inputs are the same!

INPUT A	INPUT B	OUTPUT Q
0	0	0
0	1	1
1	0	1
1	1	0

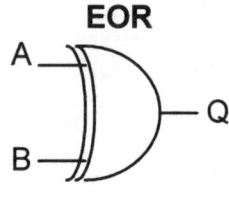

GET GOING WITH . . . AVR MICROCONTROLLERS

The NOT function (Inverter).

The NOT is an inverting function, often combined with the previous functions to produce alternative functions. The inversion is shown by a circle on the line to be inverted.

INPUT A	OUTPUT Q
0	1
1	0

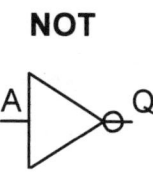

NOT

An alternative name for inversion used with micros is **COMPLEMENT** (sometimes called the ONES COMPLEMENT).
The N from NOT is combined with others to extend the functions of AND and OR to give NAND and NOR. The previous truth tables just have their Q outputs inverted and the symbols have a circle on the output pin. Since these functions are only useful as IC logic (not micros) they are not usually provided as a function inside micros.

NOTE: It is common to show inputs which are **ACTIVE LOW** (things happen when a `0' is applied) with a bar over the pin letter to mean NOT. e.g. $\overline{CS}$ is used as an abbreviation for CHIP SELECT, the bar indicating that a chip is selected only when this line is low (`0').

We are now ready to design a simple circuit using logic (just to prove a point!). Suppose you wanted a system to provide an output ONLY when a three bit number was correct and a push-button was pressed. (A combination lock!)

GET GOING WITH ... AVR MICROCONTROLLERS

Let us use the combination 010 as an example. The truth table below displays this in logic form.

INPUTS				OUTPUT
A first no.	B second no.	C third no.	D pushbutton	Lock Output
0	0	0	1	0
0	0	1	1	0
0	**1**	**0**	**1**	**1**
0	1	1	1	0
1	0	0	1	0
1	0	1	1	0
1	1	0	1	0
1	1	1	1	0
X	X	X	0	0

The X indicates a DON'T CARE condition, in this case the switch inputs can be in any position but the output is always a `0' because the push-button has not been pressed.

The truth table shows clearly that we only need to design the circuit for the correct combination, any other states will produce the opposite output (that's logic!). Where do we start? The easiest way is to start from the output. We need a device which only outputs a `1' under unique conditions. The **AND** function is the obvious choice. This will need to have four inputs, $\overline{A}$, B, $\overline{C}$ and D. The bar indicates we must invert these two (with `0's in the truth table) and is pronounced NOT A, NOT C etc.,

GET GOING WITH ... AVR MICROCONTROLLERS

The circuit then falls into place!

CIRCUIT DIAGRAM FOR COMBINATION LOCK

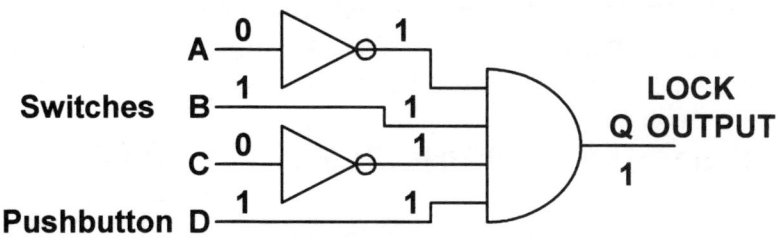

The logic levels are shown for the correct combination.

This example is a very simple example of logic design using gates. It is rarely this simple. It serves to illustrate why we use micro-based systems instead though.

What would the circuit be like if you wanted to make this a more realistic lock with thousands of possible combinations? I challenge you to design an sixteen bit (65,536 combinations) input version using gates with a realistic combination and a few chips! The design rapidly grows in size as you increase the inputs. Even if you left the specification as it is and wanted to change the combination it would mean a complete redesign and rebuild!

If this was designed using a microcontroller it would be ONE chip and you could change the combination merely by changing the program, and from a numeric keypad with a suitable display as well! You could even allow the number to be changed from outside with a password! Now you are beginning to understand perhaps?

MICRO-BASED SYSTEMS

Now we have an inkling of why we are using micros let us investigate how they function. We can start by understanding how a conventional micro differs from normal logic.

MICROPROCESSOR PRINCIPLES

If we consider a simple AND gate as an example, this produces a `1' only if all inputs are a `1'.

AND

A—1
B—1
Q = 1

The micro equivalent, processing the **AND** instruction, and assuming a ONE bit micro, would be thus :-

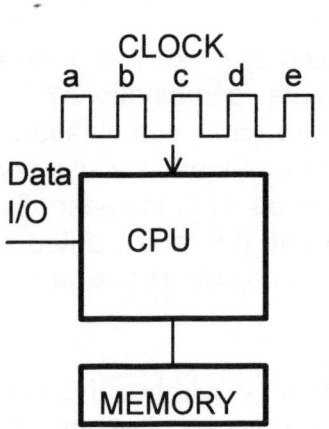

Clock edge a - the AND instruction is FETCHed from program memory.
Clock edge b - input A is read into the CPU (Central Processing Unit) via I/O.
Clock edge c - input B is read into the CPU via I/O.
Clock edge d - the CPU ANDs the two together and stores the result in a temporary store (register) usually called an Accumulator.
Clock edge e - the answer Q is written to the output via I/O from the accumulator.

Note that the same piece of I/O wire is used for all inputs and output, the data line is bi-directional!

GET GOING WITH . . . AVR MICROCONTROLLERS

EXECUTION is now complete. It has taken five clock cycles to complete a process which the AND gate does almost instantly, and this is progress? The main benefit is that in the next few clock cycles the micro can be doing something completely different, as instructed from a set of instructions (PROGRAM) stored in memory, while the AND gate is still an AND gate. This flexibility has cost you processing speed. An AND gate in the high speed CMOS family takes about 5 ns to respond input to output (propagation delay) while a micro running at say 1 MHz may have taken 5 μs to do the same process, a thousand times slower!

The secret is to use a fast efficient processor that fetches and executes instructions in one clock cycle and runs at very high speed. You have guessed it, we use an AVR!

Now is the time to look at the two main ways micros are built (ARCHITECTURE). The same principle described above holds good for both types but the way memory is organised is totally different. The architectures are named after their inventors as is usual with most inventions. The first computer processor used the **VON NEUMAN** arrangement, which is still used for most computers (all PCs (IBM types and compatibles) are Von Neuman).

Faster machines are now using the **HARVARD** architecture, in microcontrollers this includes the PIC and the AVR. In PCs the ACORN RiscPC, using the STRONGARM processor, is the only one in general use (that I know of!) and outpaces any Pentium machine.

GET GOING WITH ... AVR MICROCONTROLLERS

ARCHITECTURES

The diagram below shows a simplified block diagram of the Von Neuman architecture. It shows all the basic building blocks required to make a computer, whether it be a control computer, or a PC. (Bus sizes are for 8-bit micro!)

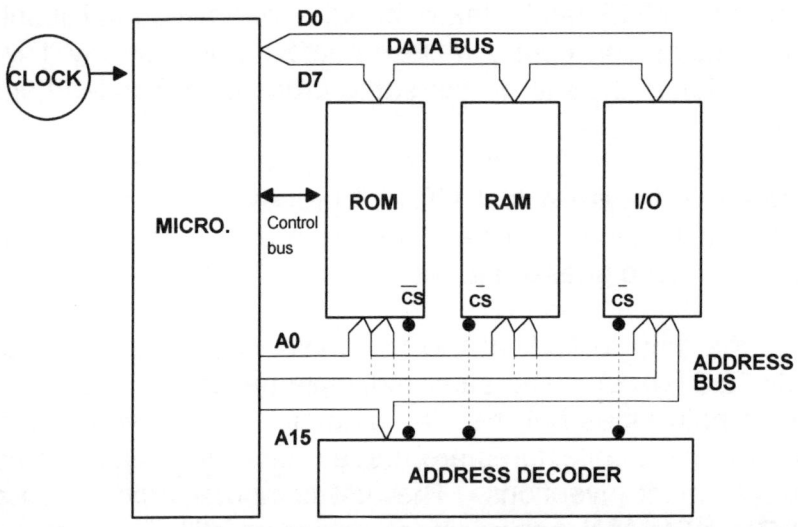

CLOCK - The clock produces regular pulses to time the fetch-execute cycle. It is normally derived from a crystal oscillator giving precise time intervals. Frequencies from 1 MHz to 200 MHz are commonplace, although micros for control normally operate at the lower end because the support ICs are cheaper! One of the problems with fast PCs is that the micro works fast but the memory to work with it will not respond that quick!

GET GOING WITH ... AVR MICROCONTROLLERS

MPU - The micro, containing the brain of the system, reads instructions (OPeration CODE - fetch) and data (OPERANDs-execute) from the same memory, via the data bus, in consecutive locations pointed to by a binary address coming from the micro via the address bus. The instruction may also require data to be written out to memory during the execute phase, down the same data bus.

Any micro will consist of three main functional blocks :-

- **ALU** - Arithmetic and Logic Unit, performs the calculations as dictated by the instruction fetched from memory. It is a programmable logic gate.
- **REGISTERS** - are fast access storage for the results (accumulator) and for other purposes, such as status indications, program counting.
- **CONTROL UNIT** - control logic to synchronise the operation of the system, taking the clock signal, and using it to time and organise the fetch -execute cycle.

ADDRESS DECODER - takes the few bits off the top of the address bus and uses it to select each of the different types of memory according to the address being accessed by the micro.
It is a changeover switch to ensure that only ONE device is listening or talking at any one moment in time. This is important since all the devices are connected to the same pieces of wire (BUS). The design of the address decoding circuit is usually the most difficult part of any micro-based system. (In a microcontroller, the address decoding is internal and has been done for you, PHEW!)

GET GOING WITH ... AVR MICROCONTROLLERS

MEMORY - stores the program and results, usually arranged in 8-bit wide (byte) blocks. Every system will have a MEMORY MAP identifying which devices are available over which address range. The maximum memory size is limited by the width of the address bus. Using the same rules as before, a 16-bit address bus, the usual size with 8-bit micros, will access 2^{16} = 65,536 (64k) memory locations maximum. For a control system using conventional micro-chips, the arrangement might look something like the diagram below.
Note, the addresses on the left are in HEXADECIMAL, see later.

The memory consists of three types of device:-

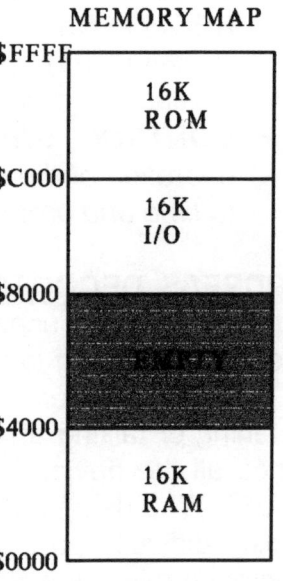

MEMORY MAP

Read Only Memory (ROM) which cannot be altered and retains it's memory when the power is removed.
(NON-VOLATILE). This contains the operating program for the system and is called FIRMWARE.

Input/Output (I/O) which provides interfacing facilities to the outside world (Peripherals).

Random Access Memory (RAM) which can be read and written to. It usually loses it's contents on power down. (VOLATILE).

GET GOING WITH ... AVR MICROCONTROLLERS

RAM is usually used as workspace. Programmes stored in this area are called SOFTWARE.

Not all of the memory space will be populated, in fact, this example is huge for control work. A few bytes of RAM are all that are required and a few k of ROM. The I/O device is often called an interface adapter and may only occupy 16 bytes in a small system.

What is a `k' I hear you ask? You may already be familiar with the terminology from PC work, but here we go, just in case! There are two multipliers used in small computing, **Kilo** (k) and **Mega** (M). They do not mean 1,000 and 1,000,000 as they do in normal science!

$$1k = 2^{10} = 1,024$$

$$1M = 2^{20} = 1,024 \times 1,024 = 1,048,576$$

Hence $2^{16} = 65,536$ is in fact 64k (64 x 1,024).

These measurements may refer to bits, nibbles, bytes or words, although bytes are often assumed, as in PC memory.
You can also see that standard decimal numbers are starting to get very big and unwieldy, hence the use of HEXADECIMAL in memory addresses. You will learn about this shortly!

We can now ensure that you know the what the basic memory types are.

GET GOING WITH ... AVR MICROCONTROLLERS

TYPES OF MEMORY DEVICE - ROMS

TERM	FULL NAME	PROGRAMMED BY	APPLICATIONS
ROM or MROM	Read Only Memory. Can only be read from, not written to.	Manufacturer by wiring in program using a mask. NON-VOLATILE	Large scale production. e.g. Operating systems (BIOS) for PCs
PROM	Programmable ROM One Time Programmable (OTP)	User, once only by blowing internal ni-chrome fuses! NON-VOLATILE	Medium scale production. OTP devices.
EPROM	Erasable PROM	User, by high voltage programmer (12v). Erased by exposure to UV light through quartz window. NON-VOLATILE	Small scale production and development work. REUSABLE a few times.
EEPROM or E^{2}PROM	Electrically Erasable PROM	User, by special programmer. Erased by application of control signal (may be 12v or so). Slow. NON-VOLATILE	Storage of system constants which can be updated. e.g. vending machine prices.
FLASH	Flash ROM	User, by set sequence at normal supply (2-6v) NON-VOLATILE	As EEPROM but easier to use and can be reused 1,000s of times.

The AVRs have FLASH ROM and EEPROM.

GET GOING WITH ... AVR MICROCONTROLLERS

TYPES OF MEMORY DEVICE - RAM

TERM	FULL NAME	PROGRAMMED BY	APPLICATIONS
SRAM	Static RAM	User in system by setting or resetting bistable circuits. (Flip-Flops). VOLATILE	Fast access storage for system variables. Easy to use, but takes up four times chip area compared to DRAM. Confined to smaller memories and high speed cache in PCs.
DRAM	Dynamic RAM	User, in system, by topping up charge on capacitor (gate-source capacitance of MOSFET) Needs special refresh controller. VOLATILE	Large memories, as in PCs. Four times smaller than SRAM but slower and charge leaks away. Needs refreshing every few ms.

Control systems would always use Static RAM for speed since you rarely need more than 1 or 2 k. Microcontrollers have this on-board usually. (The AVRs have SRAM (*with the exception of the AT90S1200*) and FLASH rom).

GET GOING WITH ... AVR MICROCONTROLLERS

I/O DEVICES - come in various shapes and sizes. The table below shows some examples :-

TERM	FULL NAME	PROVIDES	APPLICATIONS
PIA	Programmable Interface Adaptor	Simple bi-directional input or output latching.	Printer ports, parallel ports.
VIA	Versatile Interface Adaptor	Bi-directional input or output latching and other features, such as counters, timers, serial ports and interrupt facilities	Complete port facilities, parallel, user and serial.
UART	Universal Asynchronous Receiver Transmitter	Two way, two wire link, with data one bit at a time.	Simple serial ports
USART	Universal Synchronous/ Asynchronous Receiver Transmitter	Two way, two or more wire serial link. (Two for data, two for handshake lines).	High speed serial ports.
SPI	Serial Peripheral Interface	Simple three wire serial link.	High speed inter-IC link.
IIC or I^{2}C	Inter IC Communication	As above but uses two wires.	Slower speed inter-IC link.

Microcontrollers have several of these built in. The AVRs have UARTs, SPI and PIA type adaptors.

GET GOING WITH . . . AVR MICROCONTROLLERS

HOW A PROGRAM IS STORED - FETCH-EXECUTE CYCLE.

A program will consist of two types of information, the OP. code (OPeration code - the instruction, e.g. add, and etc.,) selected from a set of instructions, and the OPERAND, the data needed by the instruction to execute the command.

OP. CODE	OPERAND

The op. code is **fetched**, latched into an instruction register inside the micro, decoded into control signals, and then the operand is picked up to **execute** the instruction. The cycle is then repeated at the speed of the system clock. A program counter (PC) inside the micro., automatically increments (adds one) after each cycle to point to the address of the NEXT memory location. The program is stepped through in this manner until it loops back to the start again (usually).

In Von Neuman micros., the program is stored in sequential bytes with the Op. code followed by the operand. Some op. codes may need no operands to work e.g. IMPLIED instructions like SLEEP, which puts a microcontroller into power saving mode (*twiddling its thumbs*).

Others may require one or two byte operands to function.
e.g. for an 8-bit micro to access a 16-bit address, it must be stored as two sequential bytes (a high byte and a low byte). Any instruction which reads or writes to memory would thus need three bytes of storage, the op. code and a two byte address.

GET GOING WITH ... AVR MICROCONTROLLERS

The diagram below shows how several lines of program might be stored in memory.

ADDRESS	CONTENTS	COMMENT
100	18	CLC ; clears carry flag
101	A9	LDA ; loads accumulator
102	15	#$15 ; with number 15 (hex)
103	69	ADC ; add with carry
104	60	LOW byte ;contents of
105	FE	HIGH byte ;address $FE60

The meaning of these are not significant, they are in fact, selected from the old 6502 instruction set as used in the original Acorn BBC computer/Commodore 64/Apple II.

The important thing to understand is that each memory location has a two byte address and is pointed to by the number placed on the address bus by the micro., from the Program Counter. The contents of this location are then available on the 8-bit data bus for read or write operations. Since all the contents are merely 8-bit numbers, the micro., has no way of knowing whether the number is to be treated as an op. code or an operand! If the instruction requires one operand it will take the next number as the operand. If you made a mistake in the program and intended it to be the next op. code it would still treat it as data and CRASH the program! This makes Von Neuman micros very vulnerable to program errors.

The maximum memory is also limited by the size of the address bus.

GET GOING WITH ... AVR MICROCONTROLLERS

HARVARD ARCHITECTURE - has separate program and data memories. For 8-bit micros the arrangement might be something like this :-

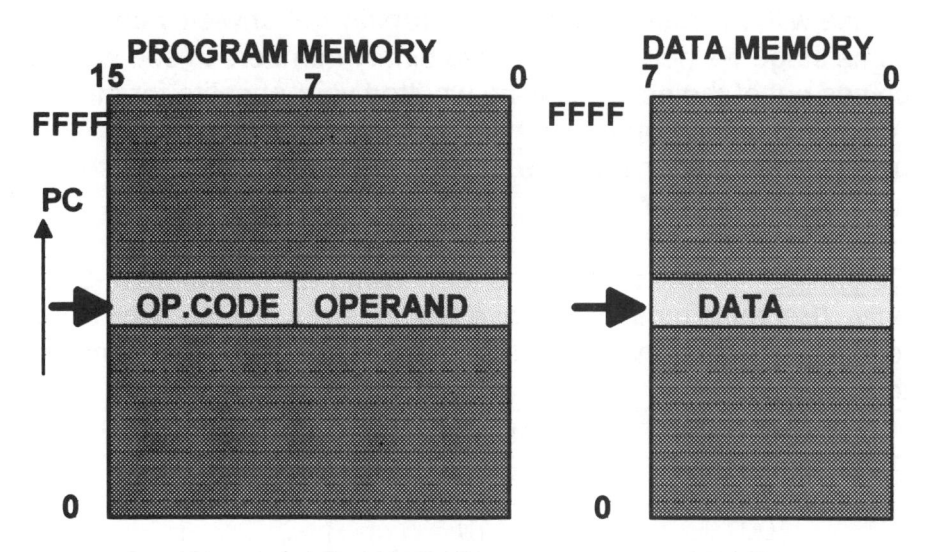

```
        PROGRAM MEMORY              DATA MEMORY
    15          7          0      7              0
  FFFF ┌───────────────────┐    FFFF ┌────────────┐
       │░░░░░░░░░░░░░░░░░░░│         │░░░░░░░░░░░░│
   PC  │░░░░░░░░░░░░░░░░░░░│         │░░░░░░░░░░░░│
    ▲  │░░░░░░░░░░░░░░░░░░░│         │░░░░░░░░░░░░│
    │  ├─────────┬─────────┤         ├────────────┤
    ──▶│ OP.CODE │ OPERAND │      ──▶│    DATA    │
       ├─────────┴─────────┤         ├────────────┤
    │  │░░░░░░░░░░░░░░░░░░░│         │░░░░░░░░░░░░│
       │░░░░░░░░░░░░░░░░░░░│         │░░░░░░░░░░░░│
    0  └───────────────────┘       0 └────────────┘
```

The program memory contains the op.code AND the operand in one wide memory location (in this case 16-bits wide) addressed by a program address bus (from PC). The 8-bit data memory would have its own separate address bus. It would usually be quite small for microcontrollers, a few k maybe. The fetch and execute can now be done in one by picking up the 16-bit word from program memory. There is now no risk of confusion and the potential memory space has been doubled! Good isn't it? By careful hardware design using pipelining techniques the fetch-execute cycle can be reduced to ONE clock cycle! The space taken up by the program is also considerably reduced. `DROOLING' now are you not!

GET GOING WITH ... AVR MICROCONTROLLERS

NUMBER SYSTEMS

The decimal number system (or denary) is not ideally suited for use with micros. The numbers rapidly get unwieldy and at some stage we need to convert to binary numbers to see what comes out of the ports! Having whetted your appetite for the AVR please hang on a bit longer to ensure that you fully understand number systems. This is important, but easy, so do not despair!

DECIMAL - counts to the base ten, having ten numbers 0 -9 only. (Because most of us have ten fingers!) We are well used to this system but may have forgotten the theory! The format is thus:-

Base ^{weighting}	Base ^{weighting}	Base ^{weighting}
10^2	10^1	10^0
100	10	1
6	**3**	**7**

The example number (in bold) is **SIX** hundreds, **THREE** tens and **SEVEN** ones. Notice how the weightings increase by one each time from zero, this is common to all numbers systems, regardless of base, and they run right to left.

You may remember units, tens and hundreds from primary school! Some of us find it easy to work in this number system! All of our calculating equipment and mathematical education is geared to this method. When it comes to computers though they only have two numbers, 0 and 1. Decimal is not suited.

GET GOING WITH . . . AVR MICROCONTROLLERS

BINARY - works to the base of two and has only two valid numbers 0 and 1. By the same method as before the system now becomes :-

Base weighting	Base weighting	Base weighting	Base weighting
2^3	2^2	2^1	2^0
8	4	2	1
1	**1**	**0**	**1**

The units, tens, hundreds columns now progress in powers of two to become, one, two, four, eight, sixteen etc., The example number (in bold) is **1101_2**. Note that this is not one thousand, one hundred and one, but one - one - zero - one. The subscript of 2 shows us that this is a binary number. It is in fact the same as 8 + 4 + 0 + 1 = 13. This shows us a simple way to convert from decimal to binary and vice-versa. Just draw the columns up with their weightings to the size required and convert as above.

The largest number you can have with four bits (nibble) is 8 + 4 + 2 + 1 = 15. Larger numbers require more bits and you have already seen how the numbers get big very quickly.

Let us try converting 247 into binary to see the problems :-

D_7	D_6	D_5	D_4	D_3	D_2	D_1	D_0
128	64	32	16	8	4	2	1
1	1	1	1	0	1	1	1
128 +	64 +	32 +	16 +	0 +	4 +	2 +	1

Adds up to 247, you have to keep on dividing by two until you get to zero. Not all that easy and very simple to make a mistake.

HEXADECIMAL - is a more convenient way to work even though it involves inventing new numbers! Hexadecimal (HEX) works to the base of sixteen, with valid numbers for 0 -15 (four bits). We cannot of course use 10, 11, 12, 13, 14, and 15 because these are two digit base ten numbers, so we use the alphabet instead :-

DEC	0	1	2	3	4	5	6	7	8	9	10	11	12	13	14	15
BIN	0	1	10	11	100	101	110	111	1000	1001	1010	1011	1100	1101	1110	1111
HEX	0	1	2	3	4	5	6	7	8	9	A	B	C	D	E	F

This may seem rather silly but each hex digit represents one nibble. All we need to do is split binary numbers into nibbles and represent each with a hex digit. With practice this becomes second nature and you end up not using decimal at all for micro work! For example the sixteen bit binary number shown below is easily converted :-

8	4	2	1	8	4	2	1	8	4	2	1	8	4	2	1
1	1	1	1	1	0	1	1	0	1	1	1	0	0	1	1
15 = F				11 = B				7 = 7				3 = 3			

So 1111101101110011_2 = **FB73**$_{16}$, try doing this in decimal. The largest number you need to add up to is fifteen. Most people can manage this, even engineers, who are well known to be people who walk around with an oily rag and a spanner!

You may have noticed that it is possible for a hex number to look like a decimal number, 11 could be ten plus one, or the hex version which is 16 + 1 = 17! Various ways exist to show this.

GET GOING WITH ... AVR MICROCONTROLLERS

We have already used one method, the dollar sign. e.g. $11 is quite clearly not a decimal number. Intel decided to simplify (?) this by representing hex numbers by 0x11, that is the hex number preceded by **zero x**! Another method uses a trailing h, e.g 0Ah. A minor complication was introduced by Acorn (who made the BBC computer and make the superfast RiscPC) who decided to use the ampersand & instead (more British what!). So $11, 0x11,11h and &11 are all the same number in hex! You will quite often see a mixture of the $ and Intel format. This is just one of the many historical anomalies found in computing.

BINARY CODED DECIMAL (BCD) - is not a proper number system but a contraction of binary allowing only the nibbles 0 -9 and excluding A, B, C, D, E, F.

DEC	0	1	2	3	4	5	6	7	8	9	10	11	12	13	14	15
BCD	0	1	2	3	4	5	6	7	8	9	-	-	-	-	-	-

Most micros provide support for working like this because it is convenient when interfacing with digit displays, a very common requirement with embedded control. So an eight bit number can now only cover the range 00 to 99, not 0 to 255 ($00 to $FF) as it would in pure binary.

Most ICs for display driving take in BCD and give out seven segment coding and require a four bit input. If you feed them illegal BCD numbers (10 -15) you either blank the display or get weird characters!

GET GOING WITH . . . AVR MICROCONTROLLERS

ADDITION - You thought you could add up, try adding one plus one! The rules in binary are quite straightforward, as are the logic circuitry to achieve it:-

$$0 + 0 = 0$$
$$0 + 1 = 1$$
$$1 + 1 = 0 \text{ carry } 1$$

(This is the same in decimal, 9 + 2 is 1 **carry** 1, i.e. 11
Consider the addition of 17 and 13 (17 + 13 = 30), in binary this becomes :-

```
17 = 0 0 0 1 0 0 0 1
13 = 0 0 0 0 1 1 0 1       0 + 0 + 1 (carry) = 1
30 = 0 0 0 1 1 1 1 0
        carry 1            Result = 30 ($1E)
```

The sum is shown as an 8-bit number, although only five bits are needed for the answer. Let us now try a sum which gives us more than 8-bits as a result! 130 + 140 gives 270, more than 255 (the 8-bit maximum)!

```
130 = 1 0 0 0 0 0 1 0
140 = 1 0 0 0 1 1 0 0       1 + 1 + 0 (carry) = 0 carry 1
      0 0 0 0 1 1 1 0
carry 1                     The result is a 9-bit number
                            1 0 0 0 0 1 1 1 0 = 270 ($10E)
```

A micro provides support for this by providing a single bit called the carry flag (the ninth bit), which can be tested by software to see if the result is too big.

GET GOING WITH . . . AVR MICROCONTROLLERS

SUBTRACTION - is not easy! We find it easy in decimal, although I can *just* remember the problems I had in primary school! The rules are :-

    0 - 0 = 0
    1 - 0 = 1
    1 - 1 = 0
    0 - 1 = 1 plus 1 **borrow**ed from next column!

The logic circuitry to do this is quite complex, making the design of the ALU more complex than would be liked! Micros consequently do not do it this way! They do subtraction by ADDing (using the same addition circuit) a NEGATIVE number to achieve the same end result. e.g. 10 -2 is the same as 10 + (-2). The number is negated by using a system called TWOs COMPLEMENT. The principle employed is straightforward, the subtractor (-ve number) is inverted (ONEs COMPLEMENT) and then ONE is added. This is now the negative version! The top bit now becomes the sign bit, with a `0' indicating a positive result, and a `1' a negative result. This is now added to the first number to give a signed result (can be -ve or +ve).

Example twos complement conversion:-

        17 = 0 0 0 1 0 0 0 1
  INVERT   1 1 1 0 1 1 1 0
  ADD 1   1+

Sign bit ▶ 1 1 1 0 1 1 1 1   this is -17 ($EF) in binary form
              carry

GET GOING WITH ... AVR MICROCONTROLLERS

This approach is easy for the micro because the simple addition circuitry is used again, switching in simple inverters and incrementing the result. How are you doing so far? Let us try a simple example the way a micro would work :-

124 - 34 we know to be **90**, the micro would do it like this (executing the subtract instruction) :-

```
         34 = 0 0 1 0 0 0 1 0        124 = 0 1 1 1 1 1 0 0
  INVERT      1 1 0 1 1 1 0 1        -34 = 1 1 0 1 1 1 1 0
  ADD 1                   1+
                                     Result = 0 1 0 1 1 0 1 0  = +90
      - 34 = 1 1 0 1 1 1 1 0         carry    1 1 1 1 1 1
                   carry   1         The carry flag should be set (1)
  Sign bit                           for a valid +ve result.
```

The micro would also have support for working with signed numbers. What would happen if the number was greater than +127? The sign bit would be overwritten with a `1' giving a false impression to your program, it would think that it was a negative number. Note, the micro is not aware that you intend the number to be signed, only your program knows this!

All micros would thus have an OVERFLOW flag to indicate to the program that this has happened. This signed number approach is important because it is also used by the micro for some RELATIVE jumps, that is, branching forwards (+) or backwards (-) a set number of places. (With 8-bits the range is +127 to -128).

We are now ready to do some real work!

3 AVR MICROCONTROLLERS

The AVR range of microcontrollers from Atmel are enhanced RISC computers (**R**educed **I**nstruction **S**et **C**omputers) on a single chip, fabricated using the very latest integration technologies. They contain, a very fast Harvard MPU, FLASH ROM, EEPROM, INTERFACE ADAPTERS and RAM. The input /output ports have high current (20 mA or so) drivers capable of driving LEDs and similar devices directly.

It is possible to have a circuit containing the AVR driving the peripherals with no other support components (apart from the power supply of course). The fact that the program can be loaded (and reloaded until it works!) into the FLASH ROM in seconds, makes for a very easy to use and cheap system which provides many advantages over conventional ROM based microcontrollers.

Those of you who have spent hours programming (BLOWING) and erasing (BURNING) EPROM based PICs will know what I mean!

It takes several minutes to blow the EPROM and a further 20 minutes or so in the UV light box to erase them. This is unwieldy to say the least but unavoidable unless you have an expensive In-Circuit-Emulator (ICE). Not so with the AVR though!

GET GOING WITH ... AVR MICROCONTROLLERS

To manufacturers of equipment containing embedded controllers (a lot these days) the following advantages are gained :-

- *Change the code in seconds, shortening the development cycle.*
- *Stock just one part, customise on the production line.*
- *Zero scrap due to misprogramming, just reprogram.*
- *Accelerate product testing.*
- *Make changes to operating system remotely.*
- *Fast processing enabling lower cost 8-bit control where more expensive 16-bit systems would have been employed. (The AVR is capable of very fast multibyte calculations enabling precision arithmetic to be executed quickly- the numbers need not be limited to 8-bit!).*

THE AVR RANGE

The range available at present consists of four MCUs (**M**icro **C**ontroller **U**nits - *more are under development*) providing very fast and cheap embedded control facilities. These are available in various package formats from DIP to surface mount. The number of pins below describe the DIP version.

20-pin AVRs	**40-pin AVRs**
AT90S1200	AT90S4414
AT90S2313	AT90S8515

These are designed to cover the bulk of embedded control applications. (See the function table overleaf)

GET GOING WITH ... AVR MICROCONTROLLERS

The table below summarises the range specifications:-

ATMEL AVR No. AT90S	1200	2313	4414	8515
No.of pins (DIP version)	20	20	40	40
Supply Vcc (min - max)	2.7 - 6.0v			
Clock Frequency / Execution Speed (max)	0 - 16MHz / 0 - 16MIPS	0 - 16MHz / 0 - 16MIPS	0 - 20MHz / 0 - 20MIPS	0 - 20MHz / 0 - 20MIPS
I/O lines	15	15	32	32
No, of instructions	89	120	120	120
FLASH ROM (bytes)	1k	2k	4k	8k
EEPROM (bytes)	64	128	256	512
Working Registers (Acc.)	32	32	32	32
SRAM (bytes)	None	128	256	512
TIMER/ COUNTERs	1	2	2	2
PWM Channels/bits	None	1/8-10	2/8-10	2/8-10
CAPTURE/ COMPARE	None	1	2	2
ANALOG COMPARATOR	1	1	1	1
SPI (program download)	Yes	Yes	Yes	Yes
SPI (Master/Slave Port)	No	Yes	Yes	Yes
Watch Dog Timer	Yes	Yes	Yes	Yes
Serial Port UART	No	Yes	Yes	Yes
Code Protection	Yes	Yes	Yes	Yes
Sleep Modes	2	2	2	2
Interrupts - Internal	2	8	10	10
External	1	2	2	2

Some of these terms may not be understood as yet, they will be covered in detail during the next few chapters.

DEVICE PINOUTS

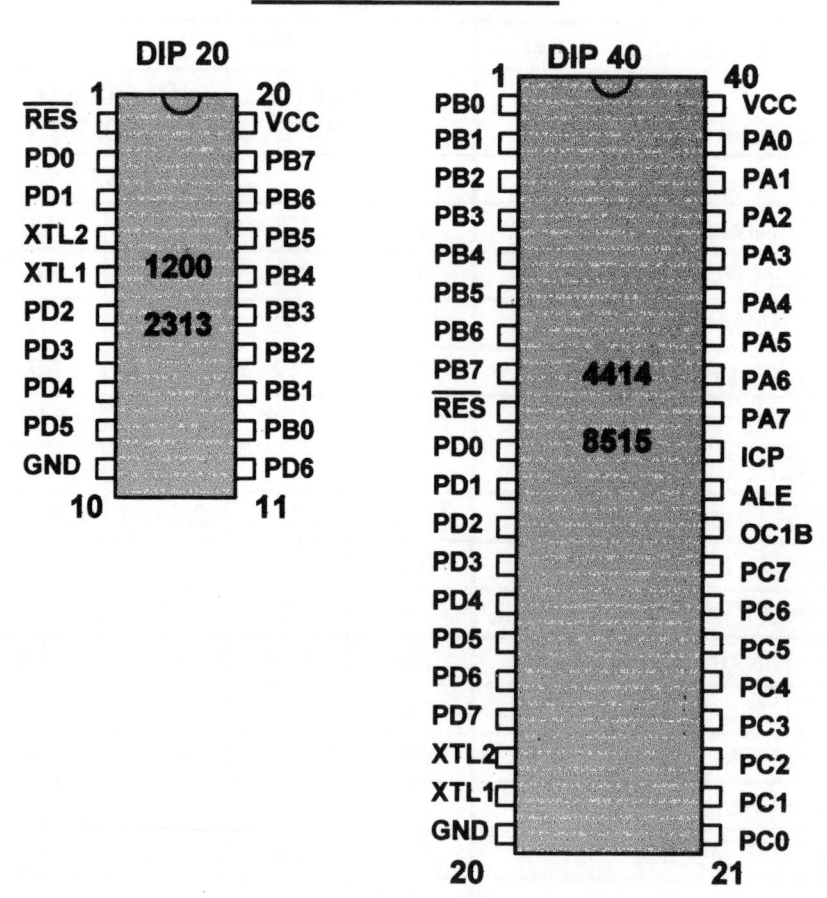

DIP 20 — 1200 / 2313

```
       1              20
 RES  [               ] VCC
 PD0  [               ] PB7
 PD1  [               ] PB6
 XTL2 [               ] PB5
 XTL1 [   1200        ] PB4
 PD2  [   2313        ] PB3
 PD3  [               ] PB2
 PD4  [               ] PB1
 PD5  [               ] PB0
 GND  [               ] PD6
      10              11
```

DIP 40 — 4414 / 8515

```
       1              40
 PB0  [               ] VCC
 PB1  [               ] PA0
 PB2  [               ] PA1
 PB3  [               ] PA2
 PB4  [               ] PA3
 PB5  [               ] PA4
 PB6  [               ] PA5
 PB7  [   4414        ] PA6
 RES  [               ] PA7
 PD0  [   8515        ] ICP
 PD1  [               ] ALE
 PD2  [               ] OC1B
 PD3  [               ] PC7
 PD4  [               ] PC6
 PD5  [               ] PC5
 PD6  [               ] PC4
 PD7  [               ] PC3
 XTL2 [               ] PC2
 XTL1 [               ] PC1
 GND  [               ] PC0
      20              21
```

Some of these pins have other functions, which will be identified as we progress. Others are common to all variants.

GET GOING WITH ... AVR MICROCONTROLLERS

PIN FUNCTIONS (Common to all variants)

GND   - is the 0v of the system

VCC   - is the positive of the power supply rail (2.7 - 6v)

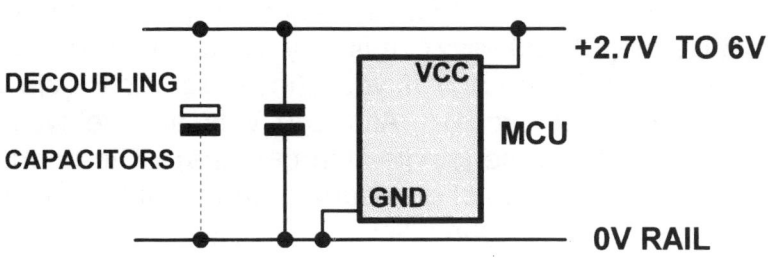

```
DECOUPLING          +2.7V TO 6V
                VCC
CAPACITORS          MCU
                GND
                    0V RAIL
```

As with all digital ICs it is important that the supply rail is decoupled with a fast capacitor (ceramic 100 nF or so) located as close to the pins as possible. If the microcontroller is to drive LEDs or other high current loads directly, it is worth placing a higher value Tantalum Bead capacitor (shown dotted -10μF or so) in parallel with it.

$\overline{RESET}$ - is the external reset line, which can be used to restart the device (Active LOW).

There is no need to connect this unless you wish to reset the micro externally (A push-button connected to 0v will serve this purpose). The MCU will automatically start running your program shortly after power up. Unlike most other microcontrollers the AVR has it's own internal power-on reset circuitry. Although there is nothing stopping you supplying your own if you want the micro to take longer starting up.

GET GOING WITH . . . AVR MICROCONTROLLERS

XTL1 - is the external clock input signal, or one of the connections to the clock crystal (see below).
XTL2 - The other clock crystal input.

The MCU can be clocked at whatever frequency you like from 0 (DC) up to the limit (16 - 20 MHz). It is fully static in operation so you can even clock it by hand if you should so wish! (Via a debounced push-button circuit). Although why anyone would want to do this is beyond me (single-step perhaps). The normal arrangement is to use a crystal or resonator in the circuit shown below, or an external clock source :-

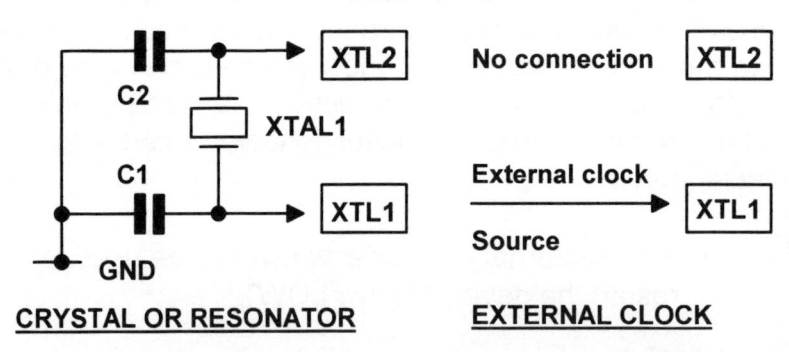

CRYSTAL OR RESONATOR   **EXTERNAL CLOCK**

The value of C1 and C2 will depend on the crystal or resonator used (a crystal is more stable). Values of between 15 - 30 pF will normally work well. If you are using an external clock source it must comply with the Atmel specification (see the data book). This means fast rise and fall times, typical not slower than 4 - 10 ns, and must not exceed the rated maximum frequency. If you are running on lower supply (<4v) rails it might pay to keep the clock frequency down to ensure reliable operation.

GET GOING WITH . . . AVR MICROCONTROLLERS

It is even possible to leave these two pins unconnected and use the internal 1 MHz R-C oscillator. (Although do not expect it to be exactly 1 MHz!) This requires that you either buy the AVR with this selected or program the device with a commercial parallel programmer. You CANNOT select the R-C oscillator by serial programming!

PXn - are the port pins and provide programmable Input/Output (I/O) allowing any port to act as output or input (but not at the same time!). (Where X is the port [A - D] and n is the bit number [0 - 7]). Port A (PAn) and C (PCn) are only available on the 40-pin variants. Port B (PBn) and D (PDn) are available on both 20 and 40-pin devices but have different second functions so beware. In common with all CMOS devices they SINK current, better than they SOURCE.

OUTPUT DRIVE CAPABILITIES (All ports)

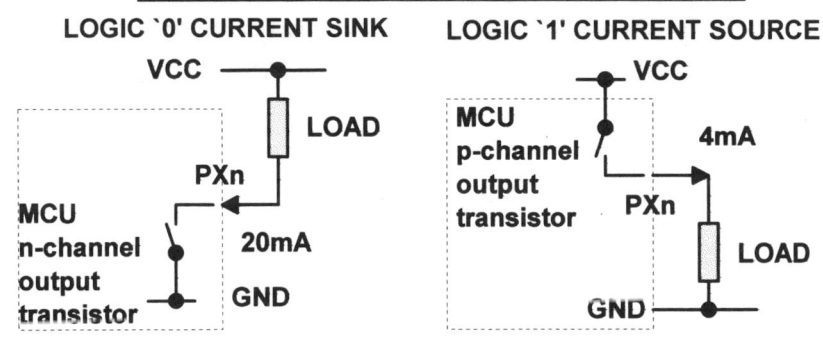

LOGIC '0' CURRENT SINK — VCC — LOAD — PXn — MCU n-channel output transistor — 20mA — GND

LOGIC '1' CURRENT SOURCE — VCC — MCU p-channel output transistor — PXn — 4mA — LOAD — GND

These values are on a 5v supply and will be less for lower voltages. You can exceed these values for short periods of time but the logic level will fall outside the normal logic limits.

GET GOING WITH . . . AVR MICROCONTROLLERS

You MUST NOT exceed the total limit of 80 mA sink for all port pins, or the maximum DC current per port pin of 40 mA! Currents outside these limits will cause the package dissipation to fall outside it's safe operating region, resulting in potential destruction of the device. (It BLOWS UP!)

PB5, PB6 and PB7 - are normally used as I/O ports but serve the secondary function of being the serial download port, to program and verify the FLASH ROM and EEPROM. (This also acts as the SPI port for larger variants, allowing several MCUs or peripherals to talk to one another.).

PB5 - is called **MOSI** in this mode and acts as the serial data input to the MCU for downloading.

PB6 - is called **MISO** in this mode and acts as serial data output for verifying the download (reading back the program stored).

PB7 - is called **SCK** in this mode and is the serial clock input to synchronise the data transfer.

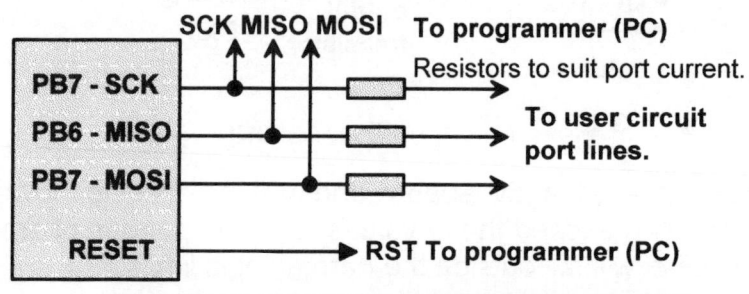

```
                SCK MISO MOSI   To programmer (PC)
                 ↑   ↑   ↑      Resistors to suit port current.
   PB7 - SCK ────┤   │   │  ──[ ]──→
   PB6 - MISO ───────┤   │  ──[ ]──→  To user circuit
   PB7 - MOSI ───────────┤  ──[ ]──→  port lines.

   RESET    ──────────────→ RST To programmer (PC)
```

TYPCIAL IN-CIRCUIT PROGRAMMING CIRCUIT

GET GOING WITH ... AVR MICROCONTROLLERS

These pins are used in conjunction with the reset line by the programmer to download the program into the MCU quickly.

If you are using the port lines for outputs, driving large currents (several mA) you will not be able to use swamp resistors because the values would have to be so small that you would exceed the safe limits. In these instances you could use analog multiplexers (74HC4052 etc.,) to act as changeover switches, or even mechanical switches (shock, horror!).

The alternative is not to have in-circuit programming capability and use a commercial programmer. You will then need to insert the MCU into your circuit after it was programmed by the PC/programmer. A very cheap and small (2" x 1" and this includes the battery!) programmer is available from KANDA for this purpose, which plugs into the printer port and uses a small 9v battery for the supply. This comes complete with programming software.

If you have money to spend then an In-Circuit-Emulator is the ultimate system to have and is available from Atmel, cheaper ones from third party manufacturers are under development. (e.g. KANDA). This enables you to prove your program, at full speed, before you download to the target AVR, driving the peripherals you intend. This is not just simulation, the PC downloads to the ICE which then executes the code on a system which reacts like a real AVR (which it may be!) You plug your target board into the emulator, instead of the AVR and it exercises your hardware in real-time (or single step if you wish).

GET GOING WITH . . . AVR MICROCONTROLLERS

The PC then interrogates the ICE to present you with details of what is going on inside the AVR. You can trace variables, set break points (to make the program stop at a certain place so that you can see what has happened), or even slow the program execution down so that you can see the system working in slow motion! The software integrates into a complete development system including a `C' programming environment.

OTHER PINS - are specific to the AVR you are using and will be introduced as we proceed.

SUMMING UP -

For simple control work the AT90S1200 variant is the obvious choice, cheap and easy to program (the starter kit is designed for this one). If you want more power then you pay only slightly more for the larger devices.

All the devices download the program into FLASH Rom in the same fashion, using the same control pins. Both 20-pin devices are pin compatible, and both 40-pin devices are pin compatible, enabling easy upgrades should you need them. The clock circuits are all identical and simple to use.

GET GOING WITH . . . AVR MICROCONTROLLERS

PROGRAMMING MODELS

To program a microcontroller you must first be familiar with its facilities and its memory organisation. The internal structure of microcontrollers are so complex that we need some simple way to visualise them. This is done firstly with a block diagram, so that we get some idea of what is available on the MCU and then with a programming model, which shows the various registers on board and any memory map.

The data book ("AVR Enhanced RISC Microcontroller data Book") contains all this information and a lot more!

If you have a CD-ROM drive in your PC it is also worth having the Atmel CD-ROM data disc ("Configurable Logic Microcontroller Non-volatile Memory"). This not only contains details of all the AVR MCUs, but other products such as the 32-bit versions (based on the Acorn ARM core) and Non-volatile memory products. If you are into `C', a demo CD-ROM of the Embedded Workbench is available from IAR.

Let us start by looking at the simplified block diagram, and deriving the memory map and programming model for, the `baby' of the AVR family, the AT90S1200.

WARNING! The following sections are very dry and should not be read without access to serious refreshment!

GET GOING WITH ... AVR MICROCONTROLLERS

SIMPLIFIED BLOCK DIAGRAM OF THE AT90S1200 MCU

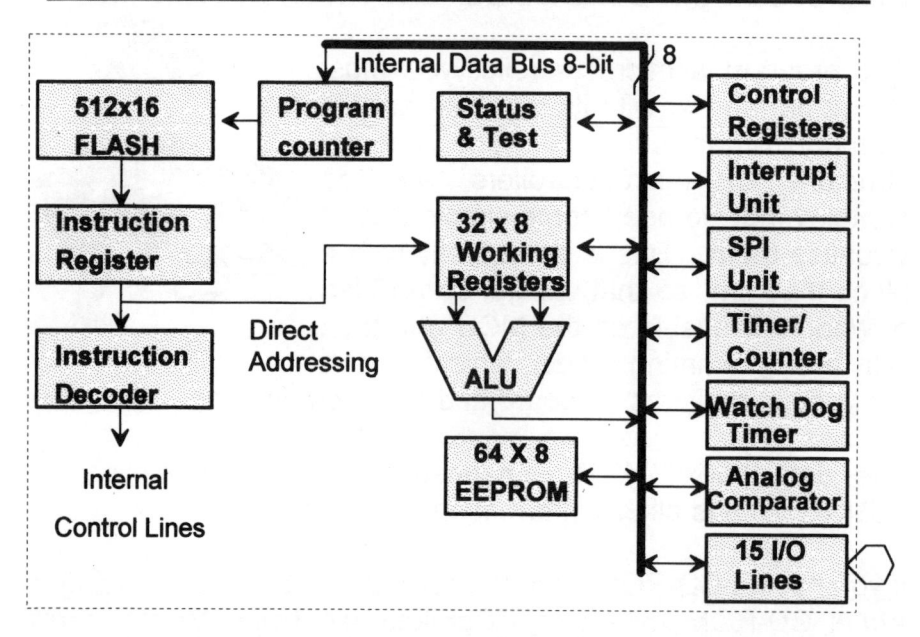

```
                    Internal Data Bus 8-bit    8
  ┌─────────┐    ┌──────────┐   ┌──────────┐       ┌──────────┐
  │ 512x16  │◄───│ Program  │   │  Status  │◄─────►│ Control  │
  │ FLASH   │    │ counter  │   │  & Test  │       │Registers │
  └─────────┘    └──────────┘   └──────────┘       ├──────────┤
       │                                           │Interrupt │
       ▼                                           │  Unit    │
  ┌─────────┐                   ┌──────────┐       ├──────────┤
  │Instruction│                 │  32 x 8  │◄─────►│   SPI    │
  │ Register │─────────────────►│ Working  │       │  Unit    │
  └─────────┘                   │Registers │       ├──────────┤
       │            Direct      └──────────┘       │  Timer/  │
       ▼          Addressing      │    │           │ Counter  │
  ┌─────────┐                    ▼    ▼            ├──────────┤
  │Instruction│                  ┌──────┐          │Watch Dog │
  │ Decoder │                    │ ALU  │          │  Timer   │
  └─────────┘                    └──────┘          ├──────────┤
       │                   ┌──────────┐            │ Analog   │
       ▼                   │  64 X 8  │◄──────────►│Comparator│
   Internal                │ EEPROM   │            ├──────────┤
  Control Lines            └──────────┘            │  15 I/O  │
                                                   │  Lines   │
                                                   └──────────┘
```

The other 20-pin MCU, the AT90S2313 is an enhanced version of this with more memory and facilities. It has SRAM for instance, which enables it to be used with `C' programming, the 1200 CANNOT be programmed in `C'! It also supports serial work with a built-in UART allowing fast full-duplex serial transmission and reception. (You could do this on the 1200 but it would have to be done in software and the baud rate would be limited). The addition of a Capture-Compare module and one PWM output channel makes it a very useful device for motor control and similar applications.

GET GOING WITH ... AVR MICROCONTROLLERS

The memory maps can now be derived from the data book :-

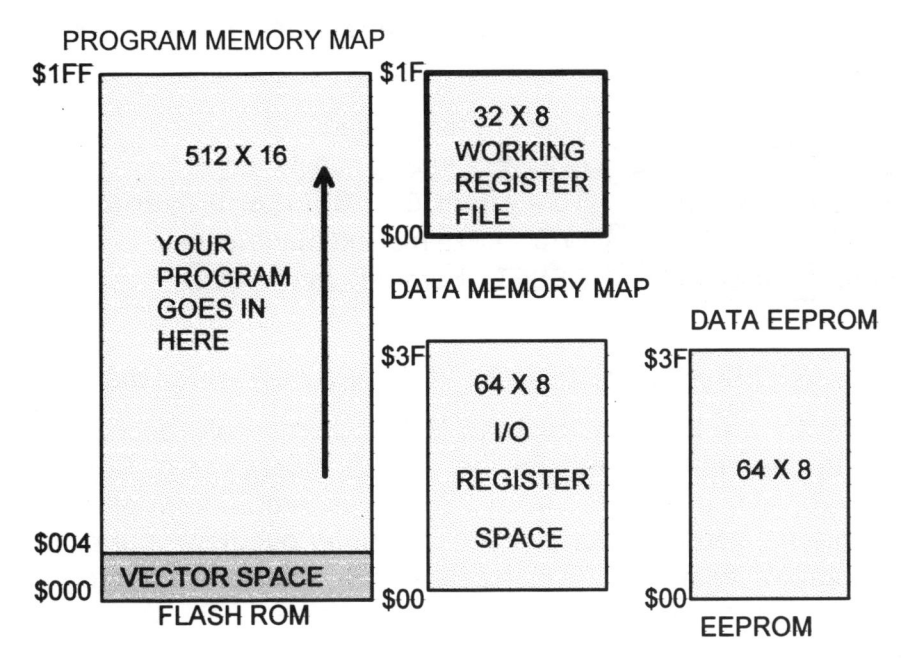

PROGRAM MEMORY MAP

```
$1FF ┌─────────────┐      $1F ┌─────────────┐
     │             │          │    32 X 8   │
     │   512 X 16  │          │   WORKING   │
     │             │          │   REGISTER  │
     │      ↑      │          │     FILE    │
     │      │      │      $00 └─────────────┘
     │   YOUR      │
     │  PROGRAM    │      DATA MEMORY MAP
     │  GOES IN    │                                DATA EEPROM
     │   HERE      │      $3F ┌─────────────┐   $3F ┌─────────────┐
     │      │      │          │    64 X 8   │       │             │
     │      │      │          │     I/O     │       │             │
     │      │      │          │   REGISTER  │       │    64 X 8   │
     │      │      │          │    SPACE    │       │             │
$004 │             │          │             │       │             │
$000 │VECTOR SPACE │      $00 └─────────────┘   $00 └─────────────┘
     └─────────────┘
      FLASH ROM                                      EEPROM
```

Each of these blocks are addressed separately (the Harvard approach).

The addresses are shown in hexadecimal ($) and start from the bottom upwards (so that memory fills up like fluid in a bottle, a cool beer will do, ta!).

It is common for this to be shown from the top down, in fact the data book shows it this way in some cases and then reverses it later on! This is a very common thing to do but can confuse the novice struggling to grasp the basics. I like to be consistent (mostly), so I have kept rigidly to this format throughout the book.

GET GOING WITH ... AVR MICROCONTROLLERS

FLASH ROM - is 1k bytes organised as 512 x 16 bit words. The bottom four locations ($000-$003) are reserved for the system vectors.

$004		Start of your program
$003	rjmp acomp	ACOMP - Analog comparator
$002	rjmp t0	T0 - Timer 0 or Counter 0 overflow
$001	rjmp int0	INT0 - External Interrupt Request
$000	rjmp main	RESET - Hardware Pin $\overline{RESET}$
	15 0	

RESET AND INTERRUPT VECTORS FOR AVR 1200

These are the locations that the MCU automatically accesses to pick up the start address for the various routines, e.g. Reset, at start up, and Interrupts caused by the external interrupt line or the internal sources such a timer or counter overflow or analogue comparator change. The rest are available for your program (508 program lines max.!). If you need more space then use a larger AVR .

The vectors are loaded by your assembly language program with the start instructions of your routine that services that facility using the RJMP <label> instruction. e.g. the vectors above are shown loaded with typical jump instructions. When the MCU is turned on, $000 is loaded into the program counter, and program execution starts from that address, picking up the RJMP instruction. This directs the MCU to an address called *main*. Interrupts, a means of stopping the main program and switching to another, work by the same process. The lower the vector address, the higher the priority, should two interrupts occur together. e.g. RESET will always respond first!

GET GOING WITH ... AVR MICROCONTROLLERS

DATA EEPROM - are 64 bytes of non-volatile data storage which can be used to house data used by the program, things such as constants stored in a look-up table. e.g. a vending machine controller would need somewhere to store the current cost of each item. This data is accessed by the program but can be changed externally or by events picked up by the program. The EEPROM can be updated at least 100,000 times!

REGISTER FILE - are 32 eight bit registers, each of which can be used as an accumulator from the ALU! One of them can be used as an index register (Z - R30) to access the other registers in an indirect fashion.

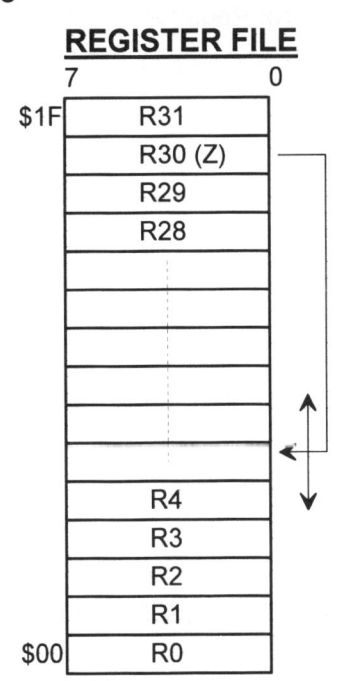

REGISTER FILE

	7	0
$1F	R31	
	R30 (Z)	
	R29	
	R28	
	R4	
	R3	
	R2	
	R1	
$00	R0	

The instructions which affect the registers have access to all the registers in one clock cycle.

Mathematical operations can even process data from any two of the registers in one clock cycle. This makes the processing very quick.

The instructions that process numbers (immediate data) from memory are limited to registers R16 - R31, all other instructions have access to all the file.

GET GOING WITH ... AVR MICROCONTROLLERS

I/O REGISTER SPACE - is the memory area reserved for the access to the special functions of the MCU and the ports. A 64 byte space is provided, $00 - $3F, but a lot of these are reserved or unused on the AVR 1200 (used in the larger variants). The ones of interest are shown below :-

Address	7 — Register — 0	Description
$3F	SREG	Status Register containing event flags
$3B	GIMSK	General Interrupt Mask Register
$39	TIMSK	Tiimer/Counter Interrupt Mask Register
$38	TIFR	Timer/Counter Interrupt Flag Register
$35	MCUCR	MCU General Control Register
$33	TCCR0	Timer/Counter Control Register
$32	TCNT0	Timer/Counter (8-bit)
$21	WDTCR	Watch Dog Timer Control Register
$1E	EEAR	EEPROM Address Register
$1D	EEDR	EEPROM Data Register
$1C	EECR	EEPROM Control Register
$18	PORTB	Port B Output latch
$17	DDRB	Port B Data Direction Register
$16	PINB	Port B pin value (instantaneous)
$12	PORTD	Port D Output latch
$11	DDRD	Port D Data Direction Register
$10	PIND	Port D pin value (instantaneous)
$08	ACSR	Analog Comparator Control and Status

The space between boxes indicate gaps in the addresses (unused or reserved locations)

INSTRUCTION SETS

The instruction set is a complete list of instructions that the MCU will respond to, (its vocabulary) try to feed it any other and it will crash. Not only do you need to get the instruction correct, but also the operand that follows it. With assembly language programming there is no leeway, it must be right! In high level languages the compiler may come back and say "Don't be silly!", if you are lucky. In parallel with the instruction set we need to discuss ADDRESSING MODES. This is the way the MCU operates on your instruction. With some micros you can have the same instruction in one of several addressing modes. e.g. The old 6502 instruction to Load the Accumulator could be either :-

LDA #$no	**LDA** zero page	**LDA** absolute
Loads the acc. with the number no.	*Loads the acc. with the contents of location $00xx*	*Loads the acc. with the contents of location $xxxx*
(Immediate)	**(Zero Page)**	**(Absolute)**

They all have different op. codes but the same Mnemonic (`aid to memory' e.g. **LDA**) and require a different number of operands in successive memory locations. This leads to easy errors in the programmes.

With the AVR each instruction has its own mnemonic so no confusion can arise, and both mnemonic and operand reside in one word of memory.

ADDRESSING MODES

REGISTER DIRECT - to access a single register in the register file (0 -31).

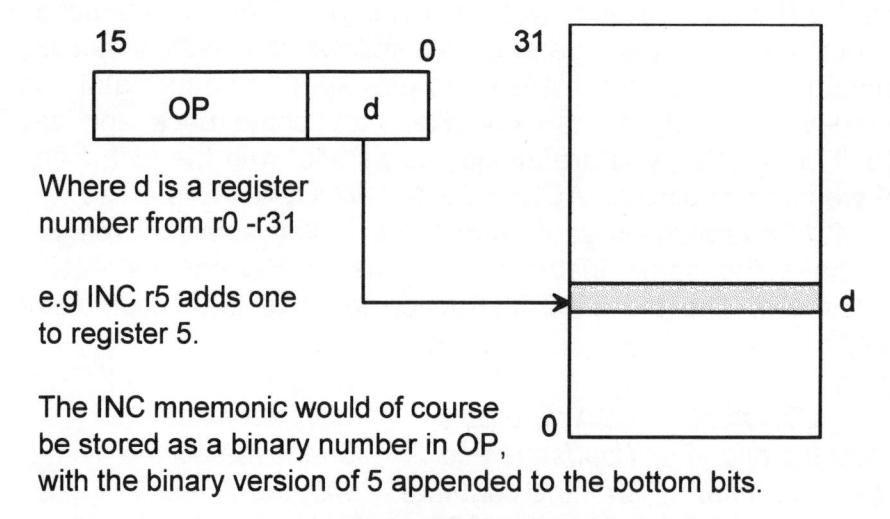

```
 15              0      31 ┌─────────┐
┌────────┬──────┐        │         │
│   OP   │  d   │        │         │
└────────┴──────┘        │         │
                         ├─────────┤ d
Where d is a register    │▓▓▓▓▓▓▓▓▓│
number from r0 -r31      ├─────────┤
                         │         │
e.g INC r5 adds one      │         │
to register 5.         0 └─────────┘

The INC mnemonic would of course
be stored as a binary number in OP,
with the binary version of 5 appended to the bottom bits.
```

GENERAL FORM | Mnemonic | Destination Register d |

The **INSTRUCTIONS** which use this mode are :-

COM - invert   **NEG** - twos complement
INC - add one   **DEC** - subtract one
TST - test for zero or minus
CLR - clear (0)   **SER** - set (1)
LSL - shift bits left   **LSR** - shift bits right
ROL - rotate left **ROR** - rotate right
ASR - shift right **SWAP** - swap nibbles over

GET GOING WITH ... AVR MICROCONTROLLERS

REGISTER DIRECT (TWO REGISTERS) - operates on two registers (r and d) in the register file and stores the result back into register d.

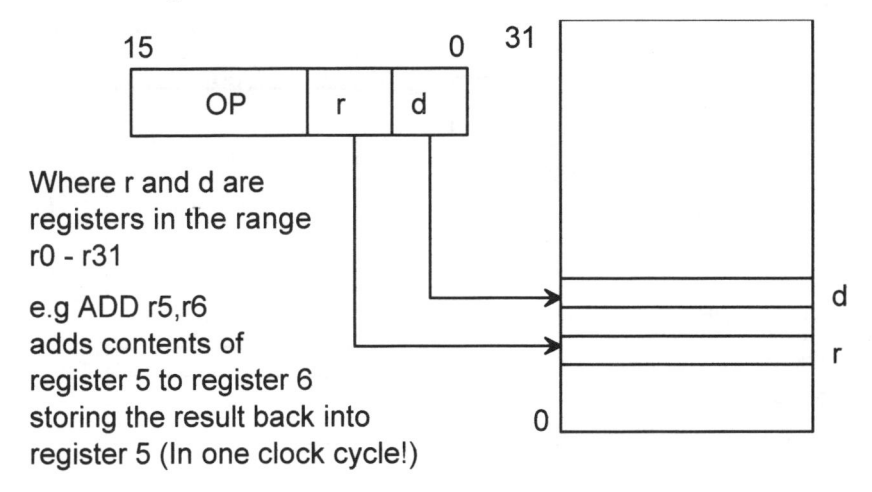

```
  15                    0    31
 ┌──────┬─────┬─────┐   ┌──────────┐
 │  OP  │  r  │  d  │   │          │
 └──────┴─────┴─────┘   │          │
                        │          │
Where r and d are       │          │
registers in the range  │          │
r0 - r31                │       ──►│ d
                        │       ──►│ r
e.g ADD r5,r6           │          │
adds contents of        │          │
register 5 to register 6         0 └──────────┘
storing the result back into
register 5 (In one clock cycle!)
```

GENERAL FORM | Mnemonic | Register d,Register r |

INSTRUCTIONS which use this addressing mode are :-

ADD - adds two reg.   **ADC** - adds two reg. with carry
SUB - subtracts two reg.   **SBC** - subtracts two reg. with carry
AND - ANDs two reg.   **OR** - ORs two reg.
EOR - EORs two reg.   **CPSE** - compare two reg. skip if equal
CP - compare two reg.   **CPC** - compare two reg. with carry
MOV - move between reg.

Note: the result always ends up in register d.

GET GOING WITH . . . AVR MICROCONTROLLERS

REGISTER INDIRECT - accesses the register pointed to by the Z register (R30). This is a form of two register addressing but enables one of the registers to be specified indirectly.

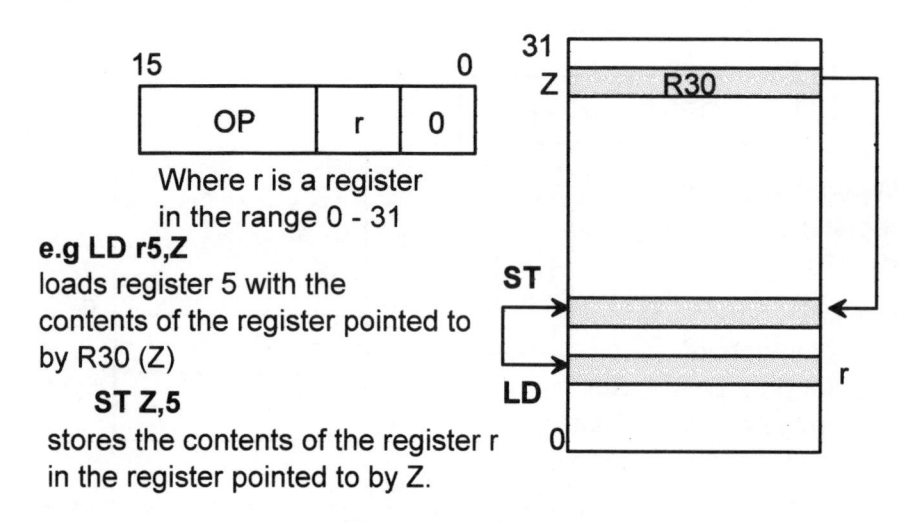

```
  15                    0        31
 ┌──────┬─────┬─────┐           ┌──────────────┐
 │  OP  │  r  │  0  │         Z │     R30      │
 └──────┴─────┴─────┘           ├──────────────┤
   Where r is a register        │              │
   in the range 0 - 31          │              │
```

e.g LD r5,Z
loads register 5 with the contents of the register pointed to by R30 (Z)

ST Z,5
stores the contents of the register r in the register pointed to by Z.

GENERAL FORMS

LD	Register,Z
ST	Z,Register

In the AVR 1200 only the two instructions shown above are available. With the larger variants having SRAM many more types are provided, along with two more index registers X and Y.

GET GOING WITH . . . AVR MICROCONTROLLERS

I/O DIRECT - accesses memory in the I/O space, for reading or writing from/to the ports and controlling the operation of the MCU.

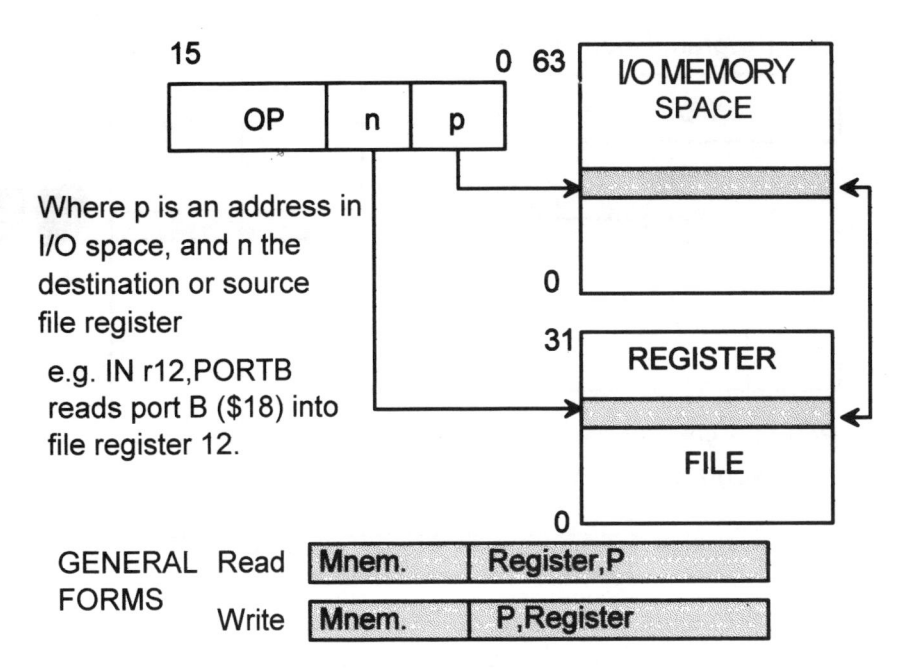

```
        15                    0   63  ┌─────────────┐
     ┌──────┬───┬───┐             │ I/O MEMORY  │
     │  OP  │ n │ p │             │    SPACE    │
     └──────┴───┴───┘             │             │
```

Where p is an address in I/O space, and n the destination or source file register

e.g. IN r12,PORTB reads port B ($18) into file register 12.

GENERAL FORMS Read	Mnem.	Register,P
Write	Mnem.	P,Register

INSTRUCTIONS which use this addressing mode are :-

IN - Read from I/O memory space into register file.
OUT - Write from register file to I/O memory space.

GET GOING WITH ... AVR MICROCONTROLLERS

RELATIVE PROGRAM ADDRESSING - uses a twos complement offset to access a program memory location.

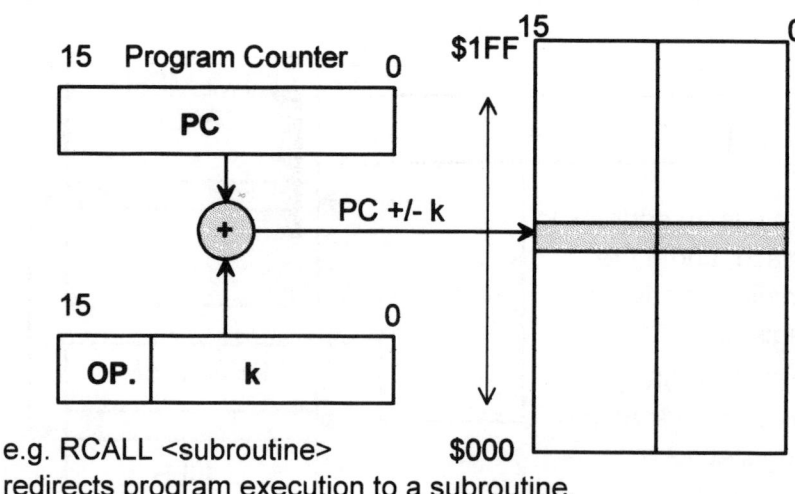

```
      15  Program Counter  0        $1FF  15                    0
      ┌──────────────────────┐           ┌──────────┬──────────┐
      │         PC           │           │          │          │
      └──────────────────────┘           │          │          │
                 │                       │          │          │
                 ▼        PC +/- k       │          │          │
                (+)─────────────────────▶│▓▓▓▓▓▓▓▓▓▓│▓▓▓▓▓▓▓▓▓▓│
                 ▲                       │          │          │
      15                     0           │          │          │
      ┌─────────┬────────────┐           │          │          │
      │  OP.    │     k      │           │          │          │
      └─────────┴────────────┘           └──────────┴──────────┘
                                         $000
```

e.g. RCALL <subroutine>
redirects program execution to a subroutine.

GENERAL FORM | Mnemonic | Signed Offset k |

Relative addressing is used to call subroutines, jump to another memory location and for the branch instructions which test the status flags (to make decisions).

The offset is a number in twos complement form, added to the program counter) PC) , and can thus be +ve (forward branch) or -ve (backward branch). Since the k part of the program line (the operand) is 12-bits wide, the program can branch over the complete program memory (+255 to -256).

GET GOING WITH ... AVR MICROCONTROLLERS

This forms a very efficient way of branching and makes the code relocateable, that is, it can reside anywhere in memory and still function the same. *Do not despair, the assembler will calculate the offset for you, all you have to do is supply a label!*

INSTRUCTIONS which use this addressing mode are :-

RJMP	- Relative **JuMP** (GOTO) to address
RCALL	- Relative **CALL** of subroutine
BREQ	- **BR**anch if **EQ**ual
BRNE	- **BR**anch if **N**ot **E**qual
BRCS	- **BR**anch if **C**arry **S**et
BRCC	- **BR**anch if **C**arry **C**lear
BRSH	- **BR**anch if **S**ame or **H**igher
BRLO	- **BR**anch if **LO**wer
BRMI	- **BR**anch if **MI**nus
BRPL	- **BR**anch if **PL**us
BRGE	- **BR**anch if **G**reater or **E**qual (signed)
BRLT	- **BR**anch if **L**ess **T**han zero (signed)
BRHS	- **BR**anch if **H**alf carry **S**et
BRHC	- **BR**anch if **H**alf carry **C**lear
BRTS	- **BR**anch if **T** flag **S**et
BRTC	- **BR**anch if **T** flag **C**lear
BRVS	- **BR**anch if o**V**erflow flag **S**et
BRVC	- **BR**anch if o**V**erflow flag **C**lear
BRIE	- **BR**anch if **I**nterrupt **E**nabled
BRID	- **BR**anch if **I**nterrupt **D**isabled

This is a very comprehensive set of test and branch instructions.

GET GOING WITH ... AVR MICROCONTROLLERS

Two more are provided which test specific bits of the status register. These require you to specify the bit to test in the status register (0 - 7). These instructions are :-

BRBS - **BR**anch if **B**it **S**et
BRBC - **BR**anch if **B**it **C**lear

The format of this instruction is :-

GENERAL FORM | Mnemonic Status Bit, Signed Offset k |

These instructions are an alternative to the previous ones, with the status bit (flag) position specified in the same instruction rather than different instructions for each flag. This can be useful sometimes, and it provides flexibility for the `C' compiler.

GENERAL NOTES ON BRANCH INSTRUCTIONS

Branch instructions enable decisions to be made and test the state of one bit (FLAG) in the **STATUS REGISTER**. For the branch instruction to work the previous operation (the question you are asking) must have affected the flags you are testing. To use these instructions you therefore need to look up the instruction set summary provided at the rear, which lists the flags triggered by each instruction. The examples in the following chapters will show examples of this being applied.

The flags used in the status register are identified on the following page.

STATUS REGISTER ($3F) - is the single most important register in the MCU (apart from the Program Counter) and contains individual bits, called FLAGs, which record an event after execution. An understanding of these flags is very important.

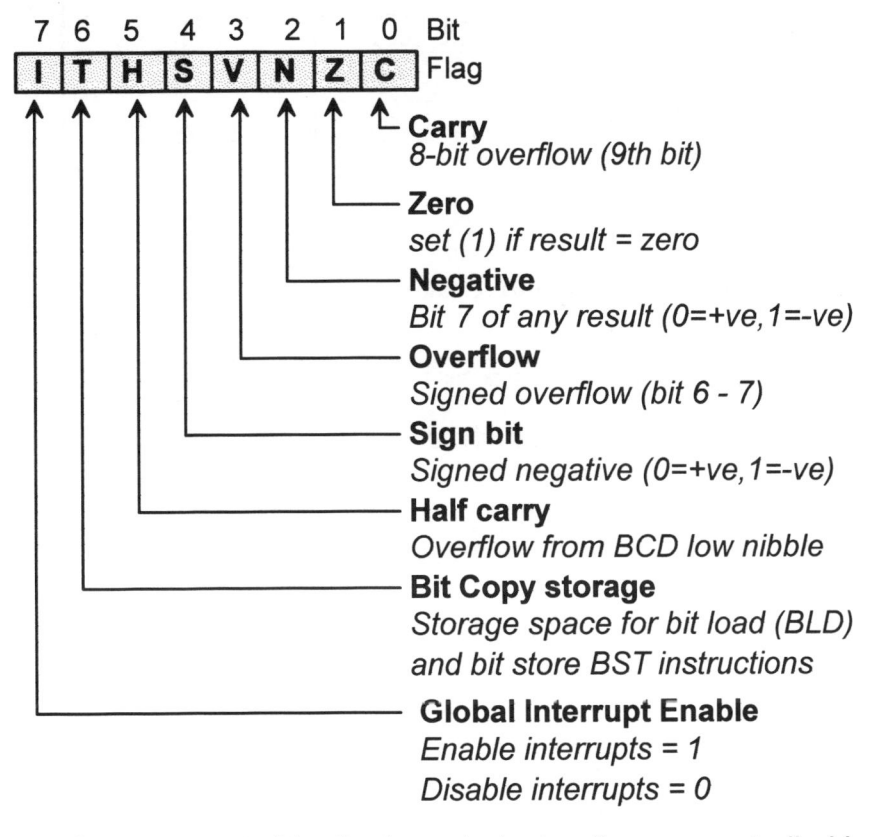

```
 7  6  5  4  3  2  1  0   Bit
| I| T| H| S| V| N| Z| C|  Flag
```

- **Carry**
  8-bit overflow (9th bit)
- **Zero**
  set (1) if result = zero
- **Negative**
  Bit 7 of any result (0=+ve, 1=-ve)
- **Overflow**
  Signed overflow (bit 6 - 7)
- **Sign bit**
  Signed negative (0=+ve, 1=-ve)
- **Half carry**
  Overflow from BCD low nibble
- **Bit Copy storage**
  Storage space for bit load (BLD) and bit store BST instructions
- **Global Interrupt Enable**
  Enable interrupts = 1
  Disable interrupts = 0

These flags are tested by the branch instructions or controlled by the implied instructions.

GET GOING WITH . . . AVR MICROCONTROLLERS

IMMEDIATE ADDRESSING - deals with numbers.

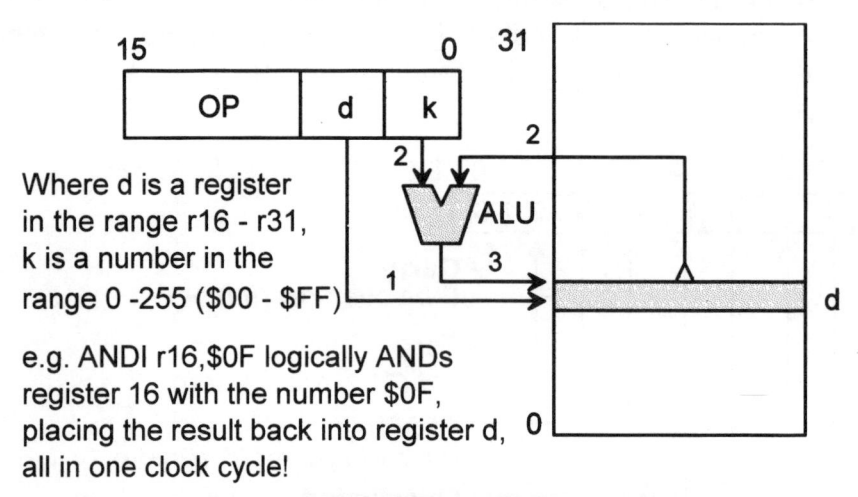

```
        15                0    31
     ┌──────┬───┬───┐
     │  OP  │ d │ k │
     └──────┴───┴───┘
                    2
```

Where d is a register in the range r16 - r31, k is a number in the range 0 -255 ($00 - $FF)

ALU

e.g. ANDI r16,$0F logically ANDs register 16 with the number $0F, placing the result back into register d, all in one clock cycle!

GENERAL FORM | Mnemonic | Register d,Constant k |

The ALU instructions which use this form can only access registers r16 to r31 and are :-
SUBI - **SUB**tract **I**mmediate constant from register
SBCI - **S**u**B**tract with **C**arry **I**mmediate constant from register
ANDI - **AND I**mmediate constant with register
ORI - **OR I**mmediate constant with register
CPI - **C**om**P**are register with **I**mmediate constant

These have no such restrictions :-
SBR - **S**et **B**its in **R**egister
CBR - **C**lear **B**its in **R**egister
LDI - **L**oa**D** register **I**mmediate with constant

GET GOING WITH . . . AVR MICROCONTROLLERS

I/O BIT INSTRUCTIONS - access the bottom half of the I/O register file to perform operations on individual bits ($00-$1F).

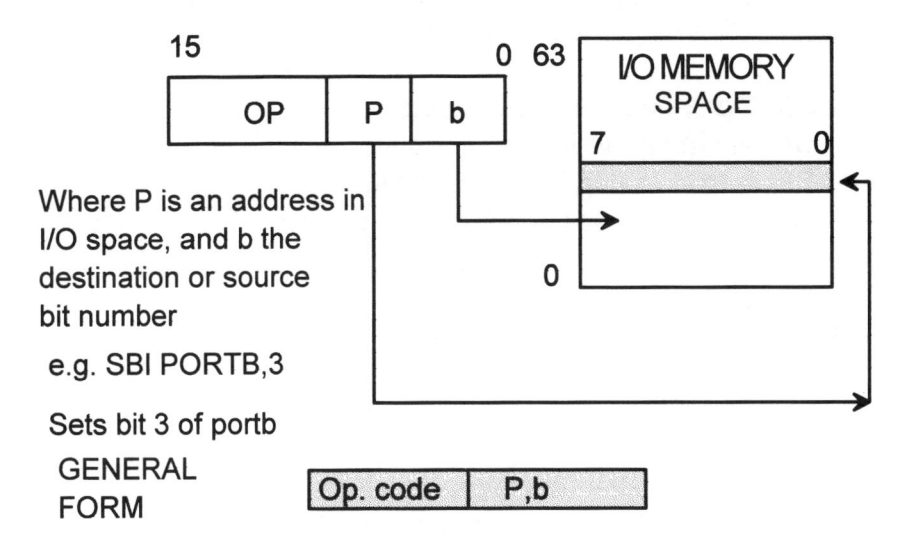

```
       15                    0  63         I/O MEMORY
    ┌──────┬────┬────┐           │           SPACE
    │  OP  │  P │  b │           │ 7                0
    └──────┴────┴────┘           │ ┌──────────────┐
Where P is an address in           │              │
I/O space, and b the               │              │
destination or source         0    │              │
bit number                         └──────────────┘
  e.g. SBI PORTB,3

Sets bit 3 of portb
  GENERAL      ┌─────────┬─────┐
  FORM         │ Op. code│ P,b │
               └─────────┴─────┘
```

Instructions which use this mode are:-

SBI - Set **B**it in **I**/o register
CBI - **C**lear **B**it in **I**/o register
SBIC - **S**kip if **B**it in **I**/o register is **C**lear
SBIS - **S**kip if **B**it in **I**/o register is **S**et

The last two test the status of the specified bit and skip the next program line if the test is true.

This provides an extra method of branching just one line and gives the C-compiler more choice.

GET GOING WITH ... AVR MICROCONTROLLERS

IMPLIED INSTRUCTIONS - are direct orders to do something and require no operands. These instructions are fetched and the appropriate action taken internally, usually in one clock cycle. The single cycle instructions are :-

- **SEC** - **SE**t **C**arry flag in status register
- **CLC** - **CL**ear **C**arry flag in status register
- **SEN** - **SE**t **N**egative flag in status register
- **CLN** - **CL**ear **N**egative flag in status register
- **SEZ** - **SE**t **Z**ero flag in status register
- **CLZ** - **CL**ear **Z**ero flag in status register
- **SEI** - **SE**t **I**nterrupt flag in status register
- **CLI** - **CL**ear **I**nterrupt flag in status register
- **SES** - **SE**t **S**igned test flag in status register
- **CLS** - **CL**ear **S**igned test flag in status register
- **SEV** - **SE**t **O**verflow flag in status register
- **CLV** - **CL**ear **O**verflow flag in status register
- **SET** - **SE**t **T** flag in status register
- **CLT** - **CL**ear **T** flag in status register
- **SEH** - **SE**t **H**alf **C**arry **F**lag in status register
- **CLH** - **CL**ear **H**alf **C**arry **F**lag in status register
- **NOP** - **N**o **OP**eration (Does nothing)
- **WDR** - **W**atch **D**og timer **R**eset

These take more :-
- **SLEEP** - power saving mode, takes 3 clock cycles
- **RET** - **RET**urn from subroutine, takes 4 clock cycles
- **RETI** - **RET**urn from **I**nterrupt, takes 4 clock cycles

GET GOING WITH ... AVR MICROCONTROLLERS

INPUT AND OUTPUT

This is what the MCU is all about! The AVR 1200 has two ports, port B and port D. They all behave in the same fashion and are accessed using three registers in the I/O space for each port. Some of the pins have second functions which are controlled by various control registers, also in the I/O space.

DATA DIRECTION REGISTER (DDR) - this sets the direction of data travel, and since each bit can be set as an input or output, you have to tell it what to be. Those of you who have played with real micros like 6502s (on which the 32-bit ARM processor was based) and 68xxx will be familiar with this technique because it is identical to the VIAs used in these systems (6522)! Each bit requires to be programmed thus (opposite to PIC micros!) :-

> **INPUT = 0   OUTPUT=1**

PORT REGISTER (PORT) - is the port contents latched in from a previous write instruction. This is the register used for outputs in your programmes.

PIN (PIN) - is the port input direct (unusual for MCUs) and allows high speed data input to be captured as it happens!

Your program should initialise the ports as Inputs or Outputs, normally at the start of the program, and then read the PIN or write to the PORT registers as they are needed. (Although there is no reason why you cannot change them part way through the program).

PORT B

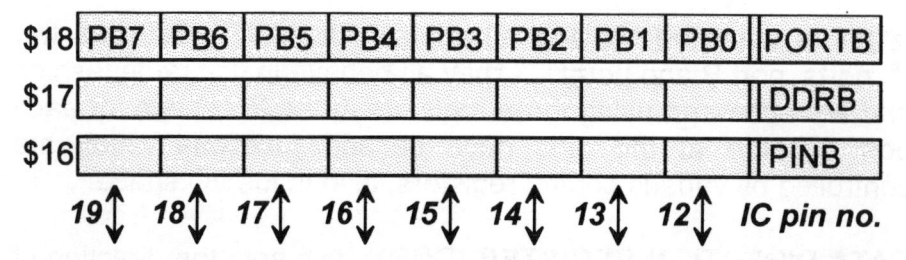

$18	PB7	PB6	PB5	PB4	PB3	PB2	PB1	PB0	PORTB
$17									DDRB
$16									PINB
IC pin no.	19	18	17	16	15	14	13	12	

Port B is a normal 8-bit input/output port, the unusual facility of two I/O registers can be off-putting, but you would use the data register PORTB for output, which is synchronised and latched. PINB is not a register as such, accessing the pins directly. This is used for data input enabling high speed data input.

PORT D

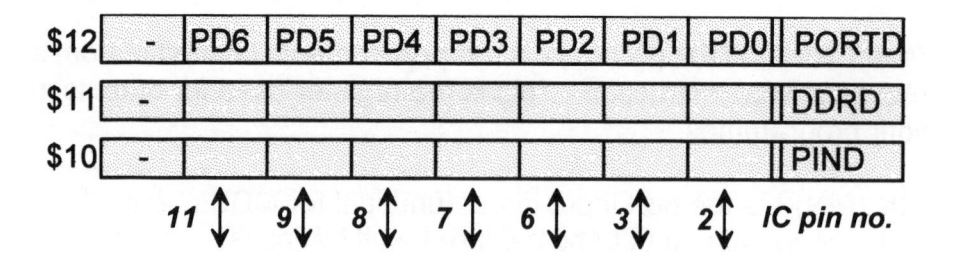

$12	-	PD6	PD5	PD4	PD3	PD2	PD1	PD0	PORTD
$11	-								DDRD
$10	-								PIND
IC pin no.		11	9	8	7	6	3	2	

Port D is a SEVEN bit I/O port (Bit 7 is not available) and can be used in exactly the same fashion as port B. The 40-pin versions have all 8-bits available for port D.

GET GOING WITH ... AVR MICROCONTROLLERS

EXAMPLE PORT INITIALISATIONS -

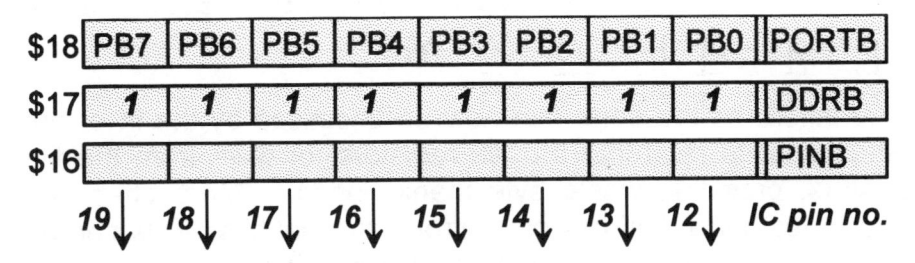

$18	PB7	PB6	PB5	PB4	PB3	PB2	PB1	PB0	PORTB
$17	1	1	1	1	1	1	1	1	DDRB
$16									PINB
	19↓	18↓	17↓	16↓	15↓	14↓	13↓	12↓	IC pin no.

The following program lines set up port B as all outputs (`1's) and port D as all inputs (`0's) :-

```
ser r16           ;initialise portb as outputs
out ddrb,r16      ;via a file register (r16)
```

The `ser` instruction sets (`1's) all bits of file register r16, the `out` instruction then sends this to ddrb ($17), telling the MCU that port b is output only. (Any file register would do!)

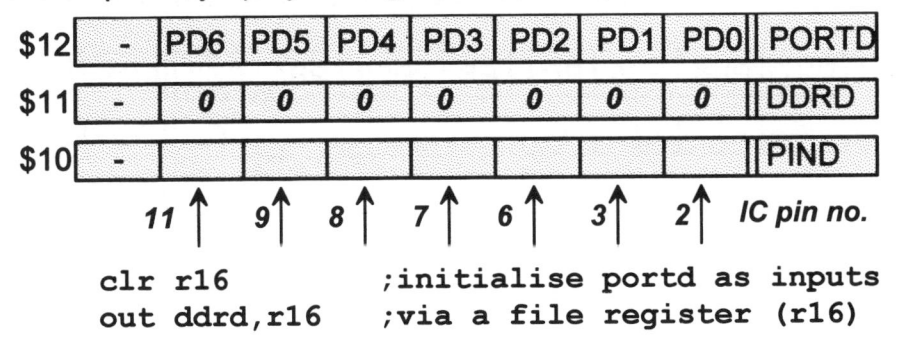

$12	-	PD6	PD5	PD4	PD3	PD2	PD1	PD0	PORTD
$11	-	0	0	0	0	0	0	0	DDRD
$10	-								PIND
		11↑	9↑	8↑	7↑	6↑	3↑	2↑	IC pin no.

```
clr r16           ;initialise portd as inputs
out ddrd,r16      ;via a file register (r16)
```

The `clr` instruction clears (`0's) all bits of file register r16, the `out` instruction then sends this to ddrd ($11), telling the MCU that port d is input only.

GET GOING WITH ... AVR MICROCONTROLLERS

It would have been nice to use `ser` and `clr` on the data direction registers directly, but only the `in`, `out`, `sbi`, `sbic`, `sbis` and `cbi` instructions can access I/O space!

Once initialised the ports can now be accessed by the in or out instructions, to read into the file registers, or write from the file registers, providing whole byte manipulation. More often you need to test individual bits or control individual bits. This can be done directly using the bit and bit test instructions.

NOTE: *If you write to a bit initialised as an input it will totally ignore you, taking up the value of the input pin.*

It is normal for you to have mixed I/O according to how many devices of each type you have connected. The following example assumes that you are using a mixture of I/O on port B, as shown in the diagram below, with one bit not used.
This examples requires the number $EE to be written to ddrb:-

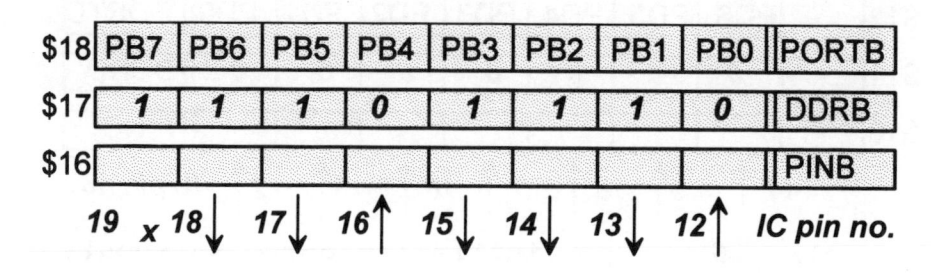

$18	PB7	PB6	PB5	PB4	PB3	PB2	PB1	PB0	PORTB
$17	1	1	1	0	1	1	1	0	DDRB
$16									PINB
	19 x	18 ↓	17 ↓	16 ↑	15 ↓	14 ↓	13 ↓	12 ↑	IC pin no.

```
ldi r16,$ee     ;initialise portb as I/O
out ddrb,r16    ;via a file register (r16)
```

GET GOING WITH . . . AVR MICROCONTROLLERS

The `ldi r16,$ee` instruction loads file register r16 with $EE (11101110) and the `out` instruction transfers it to data direction register ddrb ($17), telling the MCU that port B is input on bits 0 and 4 and outputs on the rest.

The unused top bit has also been initialised as an output so that it does not float about, picking up noise (which it could do if set as an input!).

The inputs can now be read into the MCU in a variety of ways.

BIT TEST - to check individual bits for `0' or `1'.

    e.g. `sbis pinb,0`
Tests bit 0 of port B and skips the next line if it is set (1).

    e.g. `sbic pinb,0`
Tests bit 0 of port B and skips the next line if it is clear (`0').

BYTE - to read into a file register for further processing.
    e.g. `in r16,pinb`

Reads the whole byte into file register r16 (even though you are only interested in the two bits in this case). Unfortuneatly the `in` and `out` instructions do not affect the flags in the status register, so you would need to follow this with one that does, such as compare (CP). You could then use any of the branch instructions to do a test. (Examples are shown later).

THE STACK, SUBROUTINES AND INTERRUPTS.

There are two main ways of programming, sitting down and doing it, or planning it carefully using structured programming techniques. The former is very tempting, especially when you become conversant with the instruction set. You soon learn that it pays to plan!

One requirement of structured programming is the need for **SUBROUTINE**s, sections of code which can be called up by name as many times as you like. This poses an immediate problem, how does the micro know where to return to when the subroutine has finished?

Subroutines, on the AVR, are called up by `RCALL<name>` .

This instruction is a signal to the AVR to preserve the contents of the Program Counter (PC), which contains the address of the next program line, in a special memory called the STACK. The PC is then loaded with the address of the subroutine `<name>` and program execution continues from that address.
(The AVR has in fact added a two's complement offset to the PC to perform a relative call, but this fact is hidden from you by the assembler!)
On encountering a `RET` instruction at the end of the subroutine, the AVR reverses the process, pulling the return address off the STACK back into the PC. Program execution then continues from the next program line to the one that called up the subroutine.

GET GOING WITH ... AVR MICROCONTROLLERS

The STACK needs to be quick and take up little space in memory. It thus uses sequential addressing, with a STACK POINT REGISTER maintaining the actual address in memory. Sequential addressing means that the Last data In is the First Out (LIFO). If a subroutine calls up another subroutine the same thing happens, with the stack now containing two return addresses. (This is called NESTING).

SUBROUTINES NESTED TWO DEEP - STACK USED TWO BYTES

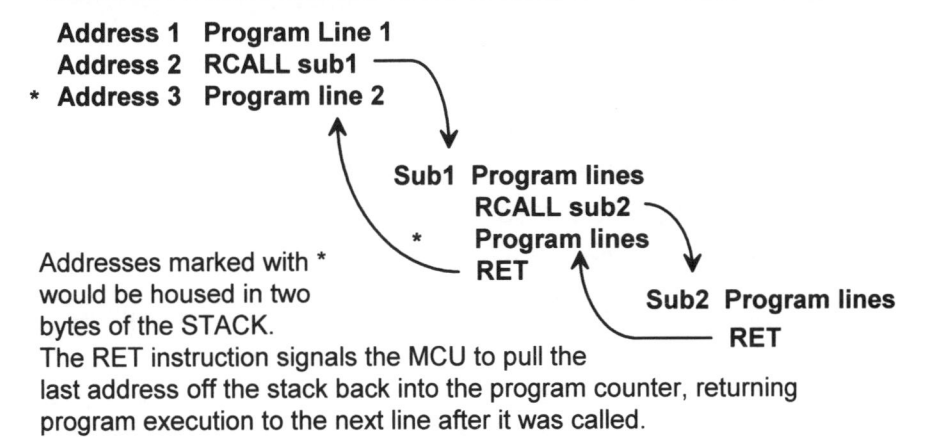

```
   Address 1    Program Line 1
   Address 2    RCALL sub1
*  Address 3    Program line 2

                         Sub1  Program lines
                               RCALL sub2
                          *    Program lines
Addresses marked with *        RET
would be housed in two                    Sub2  Program lines
bytes of the STACK.                             RET
```

The RET instruction signals the MCU to pull the last address off the stack back into the program counter, returning program execution to the next line after it was called.

On large processors the stack can be quite big, usually flexible in size, and there is no realistic limit to the number of subroutines you can nest. With MCUs this is not the case, memory is at a premium and the stack is usually quite small.

With the AVR 1200 you can only nest subroutines **THREE** deep because it has HARDWARE stack only three bytes deep!
If you exceed this, the stack will become corrupted, overwriting the previous return addresses, with unpredictable results!

GET GOING WITH ... AVR MICROCONTROLLERS

(The larger variants have a software stack, which enable the stack size to be reserved by the software itself. You can thus have as much stack as you need for the program with these.)

Another complication, which also uses the stack, are INTERRUPTs. These are very powerful methods of switching programs from outside the system. The AVR has several interrupt sources but they are all treated the same way :-

- *Interrupt Occurs*
- *AVR finishes execution of current program line*
- *PC contents are preserved on the stack*
- *PC is loaded with address of Interrupt Service Routine*
- *Execution of **ISR** continues until **RETI** is encountered*
- *Return address is pulled off the stack back into PC*
- *Program execution continues with main program.*

If you intend to use interrupts in your program then this limits you to subroutines nested two deep, since one byte will be required for the interrupt sequence! This is not really a problem with small programmes, which is what the AVR 1200 is intended for!

You must also be aware that the Interrupt Service Routine (ISR) cannot use subroutines unless you allow stack space for it. This can get very tricky!!! It is also advisable to preserve the status register at the start of the ISR, using an unused file register, since your ISR will change it, and your main program may be relying on it to make a decision! More of the tricky business of interrupts later.

GET GOING WITH ... AVR MICROCONTROLLERS

The MCU has a general on/off switch for interrupts in the Status Register called the I flag. The MCU will not interrupt unless this flag is set ('1').

`CLI` turns OFF interrupts   `SEI` turns ON interrupts

This is useful because your main program might be doing something vital at certain times and this flag enables the main program to retain control where necessary.

The AVR automatically disables interrupts after one occurs, by clearing the I flag, to avoid multiple triggers. When it encounters a RETI instruction it also automatically sets the I flag again, ready for the next interrupt. This means that you need not concern yourself with this chore.

To use any of the interrupt sources you must follow the procedure outlined below :-

1. *Load appropriate interrupt vectors with jump to ISR*
2. *Disable interrupts at very start of program (CLI)*
3. *Initialise ports as required*
4. *Set up interrupt control registers*
5. *Enable interrupts (SEI) - rest of program*

The CLI instruction must be the first line of the program because the MCU cannot be allowed to interrupt before you have set up the ports and other control registers, otherwise it will not know where to go for the interrupt service routine, or which ports do what, and CRASH!

GET GOING WITH ... AVR MICROCONTROLLERS

The Interrupt Service Routine will usually have to cater for multiple interrupts, causing some potential confusion to the AVR - which interrupt has occurred? With other processors you need to interrogate the various flags and then switch to that routine, because they often share the same interrupt vectors.

With the AVR they each have separate interrupt vectors, so this chore is unnecessary. Each interrupt source will have it's own service routine, which must :-

1.   Preserve the status register

2.   Execute the service routine code

3.   Restore the status register to it's previous state

4.   Terminate with a RETI instruction

The AVR hardware automatically clears the interrupt flag used after it is called so you need not do this. Those of you who have used other processors will find this a refreshing change! Most leave the tidying-up to the software engineer.

Example programmes using interrupts can be found in the next section.

SPECIAL FUNCTIONS

The AVR1200 has a few built-in `goodies' :-

- *Analogue Comparator (PB0/1)*
- *External Interrupt input (PD2)*
- *Timer/Counter input (PD4)*
- *Watch Dog Timer*
- *Code Protection*

ANALOGUE COMPARATOR - allows the AVR to compare two analogue voltage levels, triggering an interrupt as they become equal or greater or less than each other.

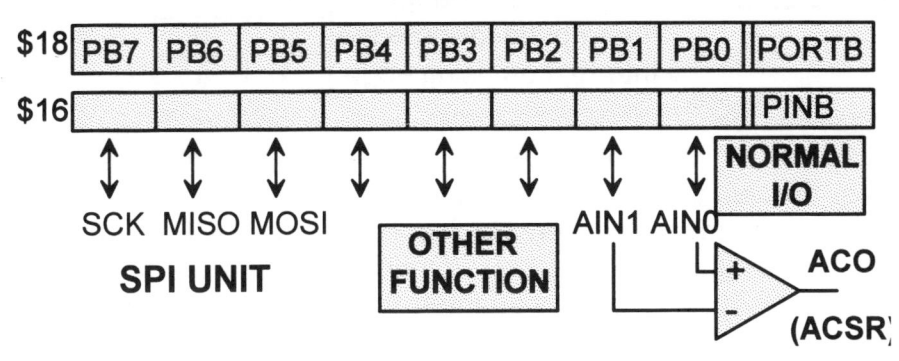

$18	PB7	PB6	PB5	PB4	PB3	PB2	PB1	PB0	PORTB
$16									PINB

SCK MISO MOSI   OTHER   AIN1 AIN0   NORMAL I/O
SPI UNIT   **FUNCTION**   ACO
                                                (ACSR)

Port B, bits 0 and 1 are the two inputs to a voltage comparator for analogue interfacing work. The comparator output is available in the ACSR register ($08) as bit 5 (ACO), and can be used to generate interrupts on the rising, or falling edge, or, on a change from either state. The inputs must fall within the supply rails, as with most analogue or digital devices.

GET GOING WITH ... AVR MICROCONTROLLERS

The analogue comparator is controlled by the **A**nalogue comparator **C**ontrol and **S**tatus **R**egister (ACSR) :-

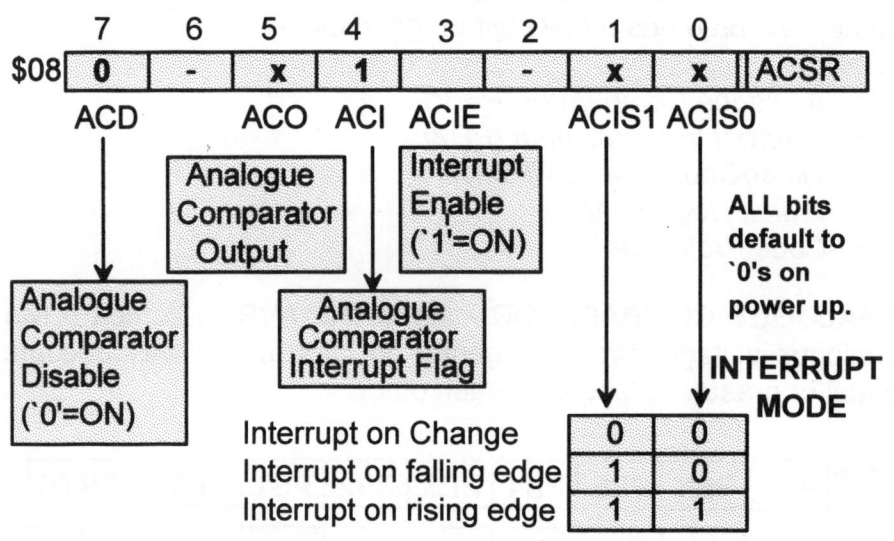

	7	6	5	4	3	2	1	0	
$08	0	-	x	1		-	x	x	ACSR

- Bit 7 **ACD** — Analogue Comparator Disable (`0`=ON)
- Bit 5 **ACO** — Analogue Comparator Output
- Bit 4 **ACI** — Analogue Comparator Interrupt Flag
- Bit 3 **ACIE** — Interrupt Enable (`1`=ON)
- Bits 1,0 **ACIS1 ACIS0** — INTERRUPT MODE

ALL bits default to `0`s on power up.

Mode	ACIS1	ACIS0
Interrupt on Change	0	0
Interrupt on falling edge	1	0
Interrupt on rising edge	1	1

To cause an interrupt the ACIE bit must be set and the ACD bit must be clear, as shown in the diagram above. If you are not using the comparator then placing a `1` in the ACD bit turns off the comparator saving power. (Only you must disable interrupts first e.g. ACIE =`0`, unless an interrupt could occur!)

The mode must be set to suit how you want the comparator to interrupt, by loading the bit pattern as shown above.

When an analogue interrupt occurs the ACI flag is set by the hardware and an interrupt sequence commences. The flag is automatically cleared by hardware when triggered.

GET GOING WITH ... AVR MICROCONTROLLERS

EXTERNAL INTERRUPT INPUT (INT0)

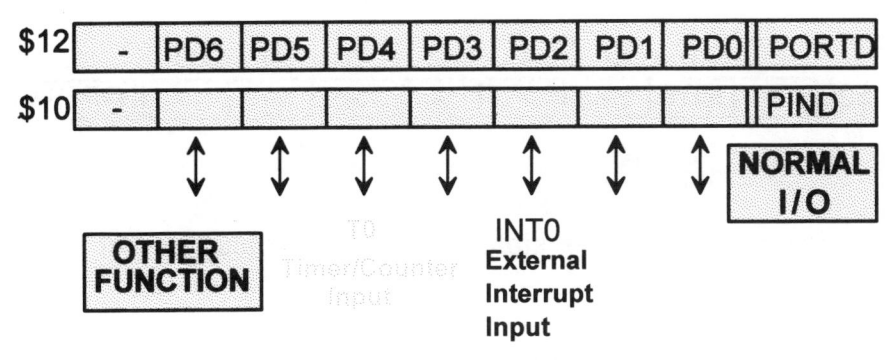

```
$12 [ - | PD6 | PD5 | PD4 | PD3 | PD2 | PD1 | PD0 ] PORTD
$10 [ - |     |     |     |     |     |     |     ] PIND
      ↕    ↕    ↕    ↕    ↕    ↕    ↕    
                                          NORMAL I/O
    OTHER              INT0
   FUNCTION          External
                     Interrupt
                       Input
```

This provides a convenient method of responding to peripheral requests, allowing an external signal to interrupt the main program. The way the interrupt works can be controlled by registers in the I/O space. It can either interrupt on a low level, or on the rising or falling edges of the port line. Two bits of the MCU Control Register (MCUCR $35) controls this as shown below, you set or clear these bits as needed :-

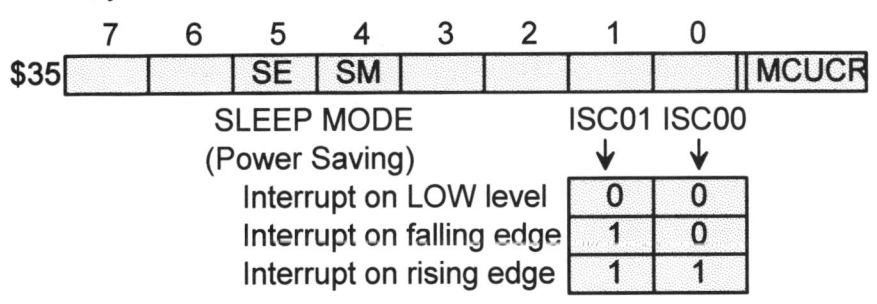

	7	6	5	4	3	2	1	0	
$35			SE	SM					MCUCR

SLEEP MODE (Power Saving): bits SE, SM

ISC01 ISC00:

	ISC01	ISC00
Interrupt on LOW level	0	0
Interrupt on falling edge	1	0
Interrupt on rising edge	1	1

The SE bit, when set allows the MCU to fall asleep when the SLEEP instruction is executed. The SM bit, when set forces the MCU into power down mode, only waking up by an external interrupt.

The interrupt is enabled by a bit in the General Interrupt Mask Register (GIMSK) :-

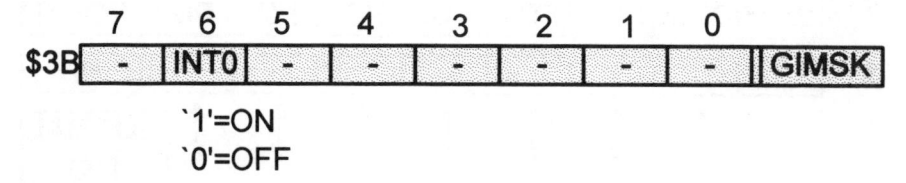

$3B	7	6	5	4	3	2	1	0	
	-	INT0	-	-	-	-	-	-	GIMSK

`1'=ON
`0'=OFF

The interrupt flag in the status register must also be set for any interrupt to function.

The input PD2 would normally be configured as an input for this function.

NOTE: Interrupts can occur even if the bit is configured as an output.

This provides a means of generating SOFTWARE interrupts, since no such instruction exists in the AVR instruction set. This is useful for error trapping in a program. The interrupt would be triggered by setting or clearing the PD2 bit as an error is detected, when initialised as an output and interrupts set up as above. This would cause program execution to switch to the external interrupt service routine which could handle all error events.

TIMER/COUNTER INPUT

```
$12 [ - | PD6 | PD5 | PD4 | PD3 | PD2 | PD1 | PD0 ]  PORTD
$10 [ - |     |     |     |     |     |     |     ]  PIND
```

↕ ↕ ↕ ↕ ↕ ↕ ↕   NORMAL I/O

OTHER FUNCTION | T0 Timer/Counter Input

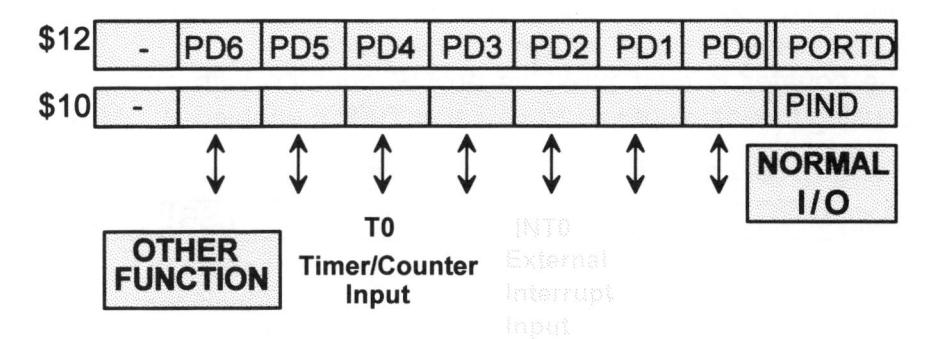

The AVR 1200 has one 8-bit timer/counter in hardware which can be used, either from the internal clock source, or from bit PD4 acting as an external input. A 10-bit pre-scalar is included totalling an 18-bit count, allowing long time delays to be generated accurately or many external events to be counted ($2^{18} = 262,144$).

The timer/counter is controlled by four registers :-

TCNT0 ($32)   -   **T**imer/**C**ou**NT**er contents,
                  A read/write register containing the 8-bit count.

TCCR0 ($33)   -   **T**imer/**C**ounter **C**ontrol **R**egister,
                  Controlling how the counter functions.

TIFR ($38)   -   **T**imer **I**nterrupt **F**lag **R**egister,
                  Triggering the internal interrupt,

TIMSK ($39)   -   **T**imer **I**nterrupt **M**a**SK** register,
                  The ON/OFF switch.

GET GOING WITH ... AVR MICROCONTROLLERS

Timer/**C**ou**NT**er 0 (TCNT0) - is the 8-bit timer counter with read/write access. (You can read the value or write the value just like any other memory location in I/O space!)
The counter is configured as an UP counter, with an overflow causing the interrupt flag to be set in TIFR if enabled in TIMSK.

	7	6	5	4	3	2	1	0	
$32	MSB						LSB		TCNT0

Most Significant Bit   Least Significant Bit

Timer/**C**ounter0 **C**ontrol **R**egister (TCCR0) - controls which source is selected, either the internal clock direct, the pre-scalar, or external input PD4. You load the bit pattern according to what you need. e.g. for a 1 MHz clock (1 μs period), selecting clock divide by 1024 (101),   means that each count is 1024 μs, or 1.024 ms, with a maximum delay of 255 x 1.024 ms = 260 ms .

	7	6	5	4	3	2	1	0	
$33	-	-	-	-	-	CS02	CS01	CS00	TCCR0

	PRE-SCALE SELECT	CS02	CS01	CS00
	STOP	0	0	0
	CLOCK	0	0	1
	CLOCK/8	0	1	0
	CLOCK/64	0	1	1
	CLOCK/256	1	0	0
	CLOCK/1024	1	0	1
External input	T0, falling edge	1	1	0
External input	T0, rising edge	1	1	1

GET GOING WITH . . . AVR MICROCONTROLLERS

Timer Interrupt Flag Register - contains a flag bit which is set automatically by the AVR when the counter overflows (11111111 goes to 00000000). This interrupts the AVR if set up to do so in TIMSK below.

```
        7    6    5    4    3    2    1    0
$38 |  -  |  -  |  -  |  -  |  -  |  -  |  -  | TIFR |
    Timer/Counter                    TOV0
    Interrupt Flag
```

The flag is cleared automatically by the AVR hardware when the interrupt is triggered.

Timer Interrupt MaSK register - contains the enable bit to turn timer/counter interrupts on and off.

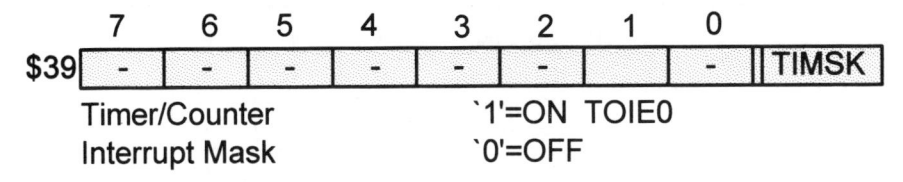

```
        7    6    5    4    3    2    1    0
$39 |  -  |  -  |  -  |  -  |  -  |  -  |  -  | TIMSK |
    Timer/Counter              '1'=ON  TOIE0
    Interrupt Mask             '0'=OFF
```

To adjust the time delay you load the count register with the number required and the interrupt occurs when the counter is full. Your interrupt service routine must reload the count at the end if you wish it to repeat.

Events can be counted by reading ('POLLING') the counter register or loading a start count and then allowing an interrupt after the required number of counts are reached.

GET GOING WITH . . . AVR MICROCONTROLLERS

WATCH DOG TIMER - this is a safety feature which allows the AVR to recover if the program is corrupted by external noise (interference). This is a common problem with control systems working in an electrically noisy environment e.g. Automobile applications. The program periodically resets the timer as it cycles through the control loop, so that it never times out. If a `crash' occurs the loop will not be completed and the watch dog timer will time-out, resetting the AVR so that the program starts from cold.

The timer uses an internal 1MHz clock which feeds a counter/pre-scalar similar to the main timer/counter. It is controlled by one register :-

$21	7	6	5	4	3	2	1	0	
	-	-	-	-	WDE	WDP2	WDP1	WDP0	WDTCR

		RESET AVR IN :-	WDP2	WDP1	WDP0
WDE	Is the on/off switch :-	16 cycles	0	0	0
		32 cycles	0	0	1
		64 cycles	0	1	0
	`1' = ON	128 cycles	0	1	1
	`0' = OFF	256 cycles	1	0	0
		512 cycles	1	0	1
		1024 cycles	1	1	0
		2048 cycles	1	1	1

On a 5v supply the cycles equate to µs but on other supplies the time will vary slightly. To use the WDT enable it by setting the WDE bit and ensure that you allow enough time for your main program to reset it with a WDR instruction inside the main loop.
You control program is now `crash' proof!

GET GOING WITH ... AVR MICROCONTROLLERS

CODE PROTECTION - when you have invented the very latest `wim-wom for grinding smoke' the last thing you want to happen is for a competitor to copy your design! When you program the AVR you can select one of three `PROGRAM MEMORY LOCK' options :-

<u>Mode 1</u> - 11 - No lock

<u>Mode 2</u> - 01 - Further programming disabled

<u>Mode 3</u> - 00 - As mode 2 but Verify disabled as well.

Once a device is programmed with the lock bits enabled you cannot reprogram it or modify it in any way. Mode 3 means that you cannot read it either, fully protecting your code from prying eyes!

The only thing you can do with an AVR protected in this fashion is to erase it and start again, destroying the program.

4 PROGRAMMING THE AVR

Now we have looked at the internal 'gubbings' of the AVR, it is time to get our hands dirty, in true engineering tradition! To use the AVR we must have a few things to hand :-

- Appropriate Hardware and Software
- Target AVR and circuit
- A good plan!

The target AVR you buy from any good distributor, the circuit you must have had in mind when you picked up this book, the software is largely free, and you must have a PC!

We will start with the most important area, a good plan.

PLANNING YOUR PROGRAMMES

The careful planning of what you do is the most important single area in software design. It is often overlooked and even experienced software engineers are sometimes (often) seen to rush into things without careful planning. The plan is vital since you get very little help from any form of software in assembly language, not because the software is poor, but because you are programming in a low level language i.e. Machine Code. You can be sure that Murphy's Law ALWAYS works, if anything can go wrong, it will. The best method to use is subject to serious debate. Most micro books use the dreaded FLOWCHART as a planning aid. I find these restricting and not easy to follow.

GET GOING WITH ... AVR MICROCONTROLLERS

DESIGN STRUCTURE DIAGRAMS (DSDs) are a form of flowchart, but are very much more powerful and easy to follow. They provide a good, compact, picture of program flow and force you to structure the program. You prepare a picture, using DSDs, of what you want the program to do, and then code it into the language of your choice. The beauty of a DSD is that it is general purpose and relates to any language! A DSD is made up from a few simple constructs, very easy to learn (although more complex symbols are available for professional use):-

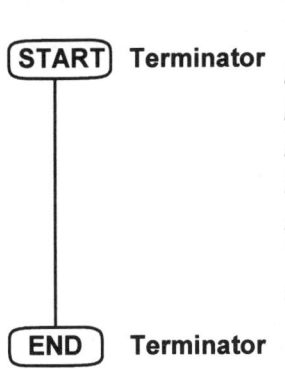

(START) **Terminator** — *The start and finish of the program, indicated by round ended terminator boxes (as with flowcharts), are connected by a solid line (unlike flowcharts).*
Program flow is downwards, no arrow is required.
The various processes now `bolt' onto the sides of this stick.

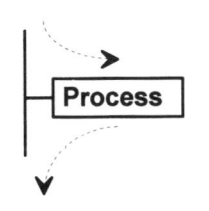

(END) **Terminator**

| Process | — *The processes are now fixed to the side of the sticks in the order of execution required. There is only one `NODE' which is the entrance AND the exit.*
The dotted lines show the route taken.
You place as much information in the box as you need to understand what the process has to do.

GET GOING WITH ... AVR MICROCONTROLLERS

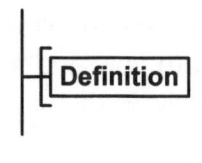

If the process is to define variables etc., then this is shown by adding a square bracket on the front.

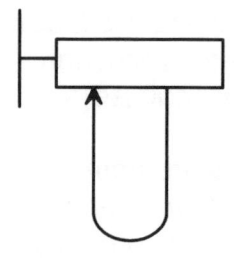

Loops are shown as a loop in a clockwise direction. The arrow shows this and is part of the symbol. The box will describe the type of loop and any terminating condition.

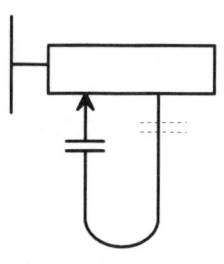

If the loop contains a test, to check for termination (escape), it appears as a capacitor type symbol.

It can either be at the end of the loop (as shown) or at the head (shown dotted) depending on the type of loop.

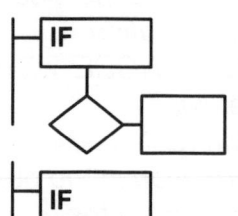

Simple decisions are shown by a process box containing the test condition. If you only need that process to happen IF this condition is true it appears as one box on the diamond.

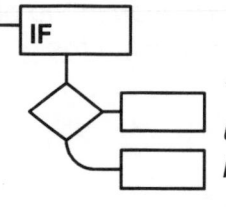

The ELSE process can be shown underneath, and will be done if the condition is not true.

GET GOING WITH ... AVR MICROCONTROLLERS

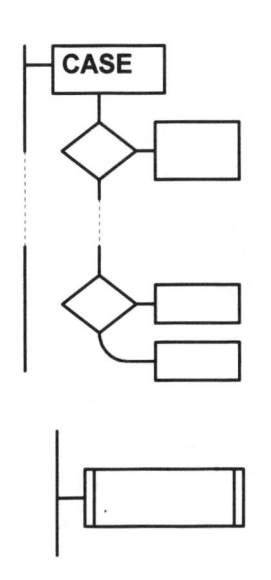

A special multiple IF structure is sometimes useful which is called a CASE structure, which may or may not have an ELSE box.

The case steps up in integers (whole numbers) and may be as long as you like, with the conditions being tested following the word CASE.

Subroutines or functions are shown as a process with a double ended box. The name of the subroutine or function will appear inside the box.

If the DSD should get too big to fit the page than the standard flowchart type connectors can be used :-

(n) From Page n   (n) To Page n

These are all that are needed to do most things in control work. We shall use these shortly in all the worked examples.

If you should wish to use these symbols for high level languages, for which they were designed, then please refer to the British Standard BS 6224 or later IEC standards which cover these symbols, and many more.

DEVELOPMENT SYSTEMS

These are the hardware and software required to program and test the micocontroller. A wide range of systems are rapidly becoming available to support the AVR range, both from ATMEL and from third party suppliers such as Kanda and IAR. The examples used in this book use these systems and will be detailed as we progress.

HARDWARE REQUIREMENTS

The first job is to have a PC (IBM or clone) of some form on which to write, assemble, test and debug the code, and finally program the AVR. If you wish to run modern software then you need a modern system, a minimum 486 processor, 8Mb RAM and WINDOWS 3.1. Ideally a PENTIUM processor, 16MB+ of RAM and WINDOWS 95. DOS versions are available for older platforms but are limited in what they do. (If anyone out there is writing a system for a decent machine and operating system such as ACORN RISCOS 3 please let me know!)

To download the program to the AVR you will need a suitable programmer. You can make your own, and no doubt numerous systems will appear in the hobby magazines. I used the KANDA starter kit, which is very cheap and includes good software, and plugs into the printer port. At present the hardware is limited to the 20-pin variants, although you can use the lead and software to interface directly to the AVR on your board, as detailed earlier, to program the 40-pin types.

GET GOING WITH ... AVR MICROCONTROLLERS

The screenshot below shows part of the screen for the KANDA software with a new project open (WINDOWS 95).

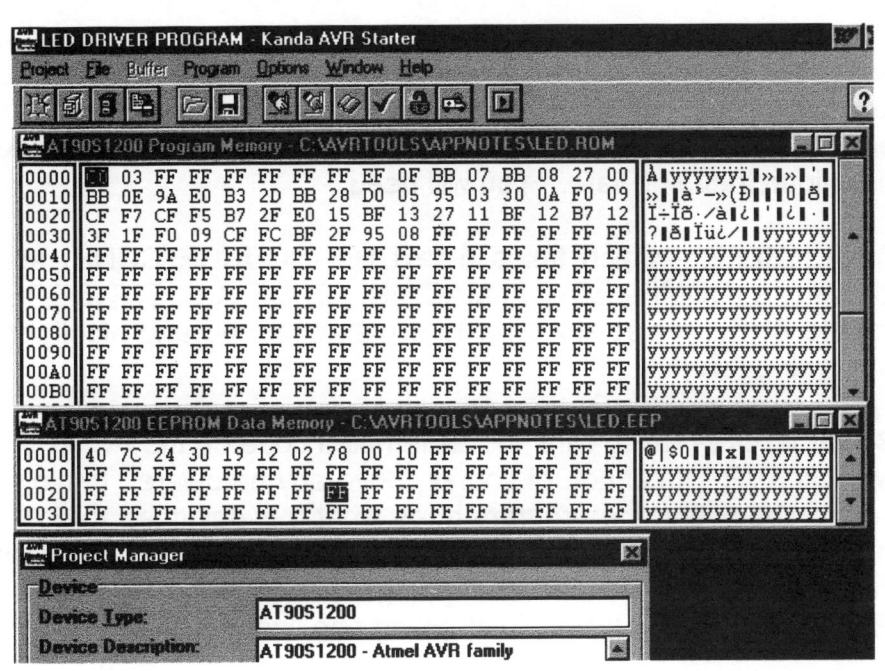

The software allows you to display and modify bytes of EEPROM and PROGRAM memory, set the lock bits and other programming parameters, and drives the printer port hardware programmer. The AVR can be checked for blank, erased, programmed, and verified to check that the contents matches your program. The software is project driven, allowing project development to be professionally documented.

GET GOING WITH . . . AVR MICROCONTROLLERS

SOFTWARE REQUIREMENTS

The next job is to acquire the development software, but before you reach for your wallets/purses, it is available free! If you have access to the INTERNET, and plenty of time, then you can access the ATMEL web page (http://www.atmel.com) and download their software. You will need :-

ASSEMBLER - which takes a text file (SOURCE CODE) and converts it (COMPILES) into MACHINE CODE (OBJECT CODE) for the AVR. It also does basic syntax checking and highlights any typing errors.

SIMULATOR - which runs the assembled code on the PC as if it was an AVR. It cannot, of course, drive any hardware. It allows you to check that the program does what it is designed to do. You can trace variables, memory locations and registers. This can be done at full speed, stopping at a chosen program line (BREAK POINT) or by single stepping one line at a time.

If you have WINDOWS 95 it is also worth downloading the AVR STUDIO software which is a better simulator covering the above plus `C' support and it also allows you to simulate the ports.
It also drives the ATMEL target board/programmer and ICE if you can afford one. If you have real money to spend the IAR Development Tools are worth buying, providing a better assembler, and a `C' compiler.

Kanda supply the Atmel assembler and simulator with their Starter Kit and ISP software.

PROGRAMMING THE AVR

At last we can get some work done! To program the AVR we must go through the following sequence:-

1. Devise the specification, hardware and software.
2. Plan the program flow.
3. Type the source code into an editor (any wordprocessor in text only mode or text editor will do e.g. NOTEPAD), and save it to disc, the Atmel version includes an editor.
4. Load it into the Assembler and assemble it, correcting any errors until complete assembly takes place.
5. Load the assembled file (Object Code) into the simulator and single step the program ensuring that the code does what it is supposed to do. The DSD will help here, enabling you to dry run the program for a variety of inputs and testing for correct function.
6. Download the object code to the AVR with the programmer.
7. Verify the code is correct.
8. Plug the AVR into the target hardware, power up and keep your fingers crossed!

The best way of showing this process, and introducing the use of the software, is to try a simple example and go through the complete procedure from beginning the end. The use of the DSDs, Assembler, Simulator and Programmer will be described in detail.

GET GOING WITH... AVR MICROCONTROLLERS

WORKED EXAMPLE

Let us start with a simple example containing several useful building blocks. We will design a system to drive eight LEDs in a `chase' pattern, with about 0.2 second between each LED display. Not very useful maybe, but it has several areas of interest. Let us get stuck in:-

The hardware design:-

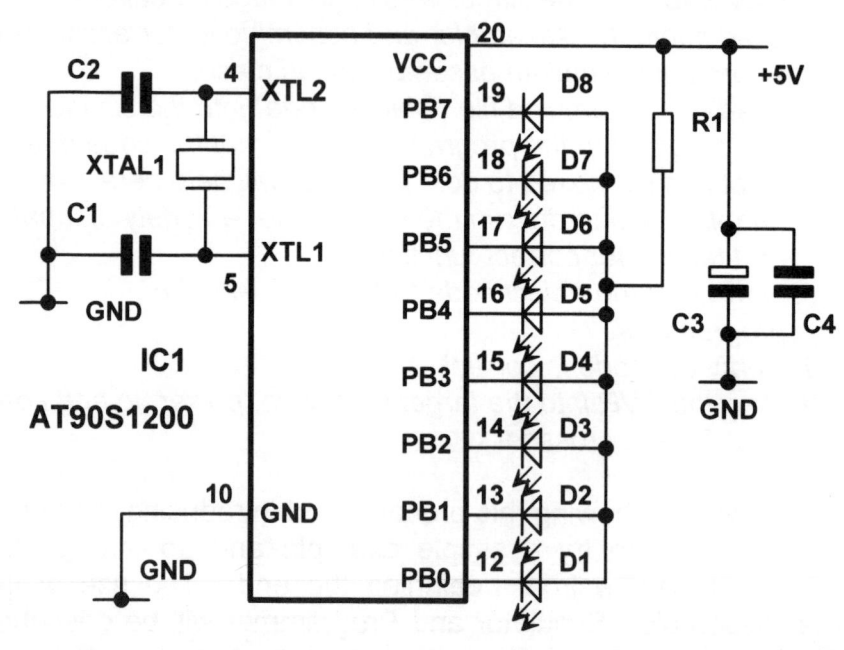

The AVR will sink 10 -20mA of current required by normal LEDs, no problem. Since in a chase pattern only one LED is on at a time, the maximum chip current of 80mA will not be exceeded.

GET GOING WITH ... AVR MICROCONTROLLERS

For the same reason we can get away with only one current limit resistor R1. Do not try this with LEDs on individually, it will not work successfully. With about 2v required by LEDs then R1 can be calculated by 3v/20mA = 150Ω. (Ohm's Law!)

LEDs D1-D8 can be any colour, and have been placed on port B, since this is an eight bit port (Port D is only seven bits!).
Note the polarity of the LEDs have been arranged so that current is sunk by the port (ON = `0').

Capacitors C1 and C2 complete the resonant circuit for the oscillator and will typically be 22pF, although this will depend on the characteristics of the resonator used. We will run the AVR at 1MHz using a crystal or resonator XTAL1.

Capacitor C3 decouples the supply rail for the 20mA current pulses and should be about a 10μF tantalum bead, with C4 decoupling the high frequency MCU current pulses, of ceramic construction and about 100nF value.

The power supply can be any 5v source or even a 6v battery.

If you have a parallel programmer you can even leave out the oscillator circuit C1, C2, XTAL1 and use the internal 1MHz R-C oscillator.

We can now start to devise the specification for the software, or more correctly, the firmware, since it will reside in ROM.

GET GOING WITH ... AVR MICROCONTROLLERS

The program requires that we produce the following bit pattern on port B (`0' = On, `1' = Off) :-

HEX	PB7	PB6	PB5	PB4	PB3	PB2	PB1	PB0	PORT B
$FF	1	1	1	1	1	1	1	1	OFF
$FE	1	1	1	1	1	1	1	0	D1 ON
$FD	1	1	1	1	1	1	0	1	D2 ON
$FB	1	1	1	1	1	0	1	1	D3 ON
$F7	1	1	1	1	0	1	1	1	D4 ON
$EF	1	1	1	0	1	1	1	1	D5 ON
$DF	1	1	0	1	1	1	1	1	D6 ON
$BF	1	0	1	1	1	1	1	1	D7 ON
$7F	0	1	1	1	1	1	1	1	D8 ON

The On sequences can be arranged by various methods :-

1. *Sending each bit pattern to port B in turn.*
2. *Loading the D1 sequence to port B and then shifting the whole byte left each time.*
3. *Loading the D1 sequence to port B and then rotating the byte left each time.*

The most efficient method is chosen by inspecting the instruction set.

Method 1 - is unwieldy requiring nine lines with delays in between.

Method 2 - the shift instruction will work but the bits just drop off the end when shifted left.

Method 3 - the rotate instruction recycles the byte through the carry flag, just right!

GET GOING WITH ... AVR MICROCONTROLLERS

If we set all bits in a file register and clear the carry flag, then each rotate left instruction (ROL) will produce exactly the sequence we need. (Refer to the instruction set at the back!)

Firmware Specification :-

1. Initialise port B as outputs
2. Blank all LEDs (11111111 to port B)
3. Clear carry flag
4. Load file register with 1's
5. Send to port B
6. Delay 0.2s (Subroutine)
7. Rotate file register left
8. Go to 5.

We can now show this in a DSD :-

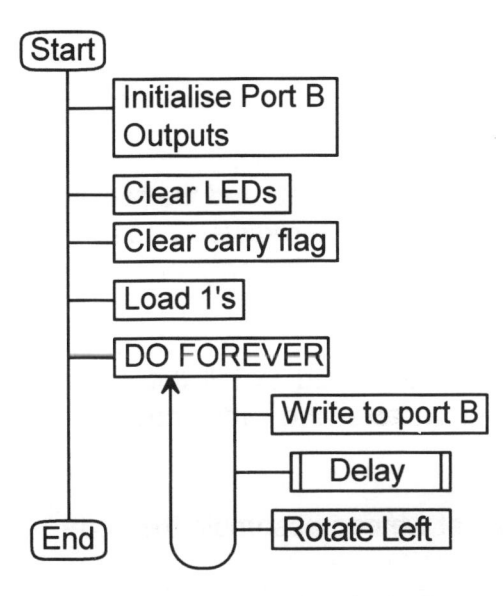

```
[Start]
   ├─[Initialise Port B Outputs]
   ├─[Clear LEDs]
   ├─[Clear carry flag]
   ├─[Load 1's]
   ├─[DO FOREVER]
   │     ├─[Write to port B]
   │     ├─[Delay]
   │     └─[Rotate Left]
[End]
```

The program flow is clearly visible, with the one off processes out of the continuous loop.

You can `dry run' the process on a piece of paper and check that it functions.

The delay will need to be a subroutine that we will sort out later. This is a good approach, one problem at a time.

GET GOING WITH ... AVR MICROCONTROLLERS

We can now code this DSD, neglecting the delay for the time being. The source code is shown below, alongside the simplified DSD to enable you to see the method of conversion :-

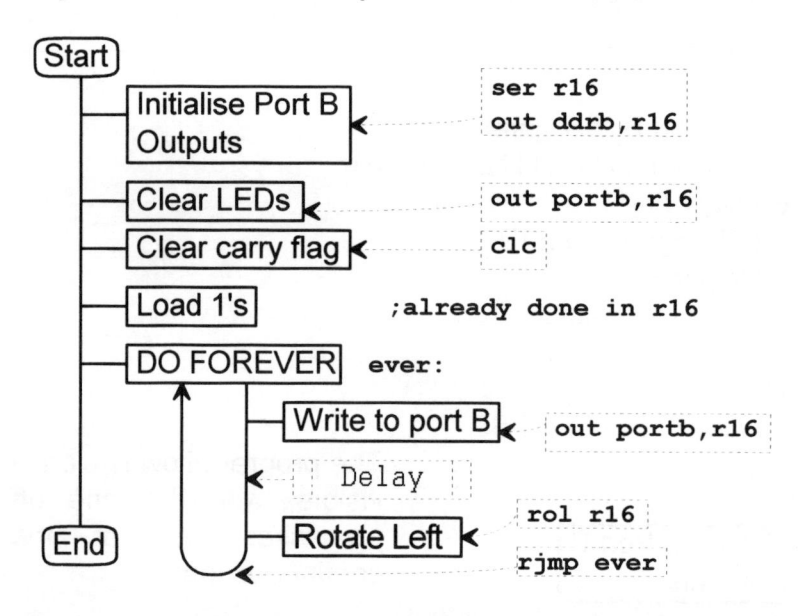

```
Start
 │
 ├─ Initialise Port B Outputs ◄──── ser r16
 │                                  out ddrb,r16
 │
 ├─ Clear LEDs ◄─────────────────── out portb,r16
 │
 ├─ Clear carry flag ◄───────────── clc
 │
 ├─ Load 1's              ;already done in r16
 │
 ├─ DO FOREVER            ever:
 │      │
 │      ├─ Write to port B ◄─────── out portb,r16
 │      │
 │      ├─ Delay
 │      │
 │      ├─ Rotate Left ◄──────────── rol r16
 │      │                            rjmp ever
 │      └──────────┘
 │
End
```

The code is derived from the instruction set, and file register r16 was chosen at random, it could be any file register 0 - 31.
(Be careful though, registers 16-31 are the only ones you can use for Immediate addressing LDI etc.,)

This is not ready to type in yet, we need to tell the assembler what to do, set up labels and vectors and other housekeeping chores.

This we must look at next so that we can assemble the code.

GET GOING WITH ... AVR MICROCONTROLLERS

Source Code Preparation - using the assembler.

The assembler takes in a text file and processes it compiling it into pure machine code. It does more than this though. It provides support for the programmer in a variety of ways :-

- It allows the use of labels instead of specifying addresses, or calculating relative offsets, making the program easier to read and follow. It substitutes the addresses and calculates relative offsets in the object code for you (this saves you lots of 2's complement work!).
- It checks syntax, the assembly language format, and tells you if it cannot understand something.
- It allows you to write commonly used routines (MACROS) and save them to a library. These can then be called up in any of your main programmes requiring them and linked at assembly time, inserting the code, thus saving you writing them again.
- It organises file listings for you, providing a choice of printout styles
- It allows assembly time expressions to be evaluated enabling programmes to be customised during assembly.

The WINDOWS version of the Atmel assembler also includes a built-in text editor which is a bonus.

Assemblers all look very similar, only the odd syntax methods occasionally catch you out.

GET GOING WITH... AVR MICROCONTROLLERS

<u>Assembler Directives</u> - do not create any code, but tell the assembler what to do. Such things as where to put the program in memory, what the labels mean, and defining and calling up Macros. The ones shown below are a small selection from the Atmel assembler, enough to get us going, and they all start with a full stop (.), others will be introduced as we progress :-

.org <address>   -   *tells the assembler where to start putting the code.*

.equ label = <address> - *tells the assembler to substitute the address for the label during assembly.*

.def label =<register no.> - *tells the assembler to use the register number every time it sees the label.*

Labels or symbols are defined with a colon on the end (e.g. `start:`) and called up as the operand by the name only (e.g `rjmp start`). The source code is typed in three main fields, separated by at least a space or even a <tab> :-

```
<Address> <instruction>        ;comment
;##########title of program##############
           .org $000           ;bottom of memory
           .equ portb =$18;port B address
start:     ser r16             ;load r16 with all 1's
```

Anything after a semi-colon is ignored by the assembler so can be used to comment the program to make it more readable, as shown in the examples above. Now we can type in our source code.

GET GOING WITH ... AVR MICROCONTROLLERS

Run the Atmel assembler **wavrasm**, click on **file** and select **new**. You can now start typing as shown below :-

```
;##################################################
;#      Example program to drive 8 LEDs in a      #
;#      chase pattern.                            #
;#      Target processor AT90S1200                #
;#      Written: Peter Sharpe 25/7/97 Ver. 1.0    #
;##################################################
            .equ ddrb =$17    ;define data direction
            .equ portb=$18    ;and port registers
            .def led =r16     ;define r16 as led
            .org $000         ;reset vector in ROM
reset:      rjmp start        ;jump to main program
            .org $004         ;first free ROM space
start:      ser led           ;initialise port B as
            out ddrb,led      ;all outputs
            out portb,led     ;clear LEDs
            clc               ;ensure carry bit=0
ever:          out portb,led    ;write to LEDs
               rol led           ;rotate byte left x1
            rjmp ever
```

Now save the file with **save as** and type in a file name, I used **chase.asm**. To assemble the program click on **assemble** and a window should open telling you of any errors. Select **WINDOW**, and **Tile Vertical** to display the two side-by-side.
If there are any errors reported, clicking on the error line will highlight the line with the error in and tell you what is wrong. Correct the typing error (which it must be!) and try again. It is worth setting up the options to save before assembly, ensuring that you always have an up-to-date copy of the file on disc.

GET GOING WITH . . . AVR MICROCONTROLLERS

NOTES: The assembler is not fussy about positioning of spaces and operators. You set your own style. Some people like to keep the variable names in upper case and instructions in lower case. This requires more keyboarding skills, makes the program easier to follow maybe, but makes no difference to the program.

The program includes a title box commented out. The format is a matter of personal style, but it should be there to tell you what the program does. Individual program lines are also commented as a narrative, and should match the wording of the DSD.

The forever loop is indented to make it show up as a loop. This is a good habit to get into since it makes the program easier to follow.

Simulation - we are now ready to test the program on the simulator. The assembler will have created an object file with a .obj extension, in our case called `chase.obj`. Run the simulator `wavrsim` and open the object file. Set up the simulator to view registers with `View - registers`, set up the options with `Options - AVR - AT90S1200`, `Options - simulator - update windows` and untick display in decimal. Now tile the windows vertically and you are ready to go. This set-up will be remembered next time you use it.

You can now single step the program by clicking on `Debug - Trace into`, and then clicking on the `CALL` icon to step each line at a time.

Try this and you will see the registers updating each time.

GET GOING WITH . . . AVR MICROCONTROLLERS

Things to look for :-

*Reset vector working
PC incrementing,
Status bits changing
r16 going through the sequence (page 94)*

Unfortunately this software does not show the ports (at least the version I had did not!), AVR STUDIO does.

Now run the program with **Debug** - **Run** and you will see the program cycling around the forever loop. You will also see why we need a delay between each output. The loop is only three cycles long so at 1MHz the LEDs will cycle every 3 μs! You will not see this (even through rose coloured glasses!).

If you have trouble with the software refer to the user manuals which are very good. These are provided on the CD-ROM and are also available from ATMEL. If you use WINDOWS regularly then you should have no problems, with most functions being obvious/intuitive.

It is not worth programming the AVR yet because execution is too quick. We need to slow it down! This requires a delay subroutine which is the next stage.

GET GOING WITH ... AVR MICROCONTROLLERS

<u>Time Delay Subroutine</u> - needs to waste about 0.2 s to enable us the see the LED flash. This can be achieved by several methods:-

- use NOP instructions to waste clock cycles.
- use the internal timer/pre-scalar.
- make a nested time waste loop, using file registers as counters.

The NOP instruction does nothing except waste one clock cycle (1 μs), so you would require 200,000 of these! A liitle wasteful!

The internal timer/counter can use the 1 MHz system clock to time events. This could be used, but involves interrupts or polling, which we are not quite ready for yet, and it is much too easy anyway!

To make a time waste loop we need to use a counter and construct a FOR loop, which repeats a loop a set number of times. Any file register will do, except r16 which we are using already. The DSD and section of program below shows how a simple one loop time waste loop can be constructed:-

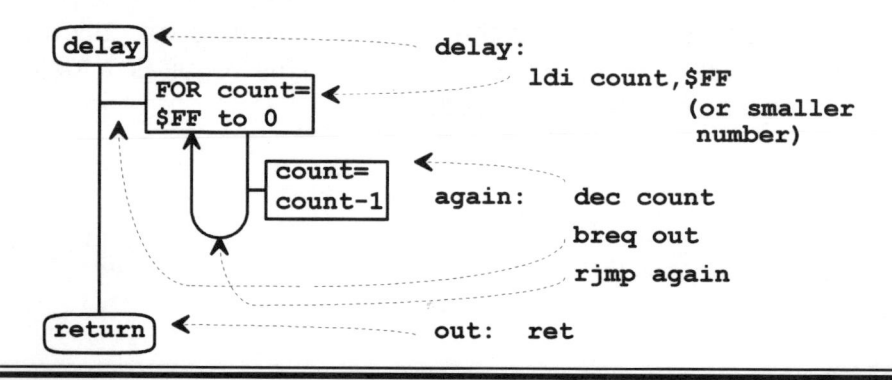

```
                              delay:
                                   ldi count,$FF
                                        (or smaller
                                         number)

                              again: dec count
                                     breq out
                                     rjmp again

                              out:   ret
```

GET GOING WITH ... AVR MICROCONTROLLERS

This routine loads a register, which we will need to define, called count, with a number. The size of the number will dictate how many times it goes round the loop. The counter is decremented each time round the loop with `dec count` and tested for zero with a Branch if Equal instruction `breq`. If the counter is not zero the branch will not be taken and the loop repeats with `rjmp again`. When the counter falls to zero after the `dec` instruction the Z flag will be set and the branch will be taken, taking the program out of the loop, picking up the `ret` instruction, which directs the program back to the next line after the subroutine was called.

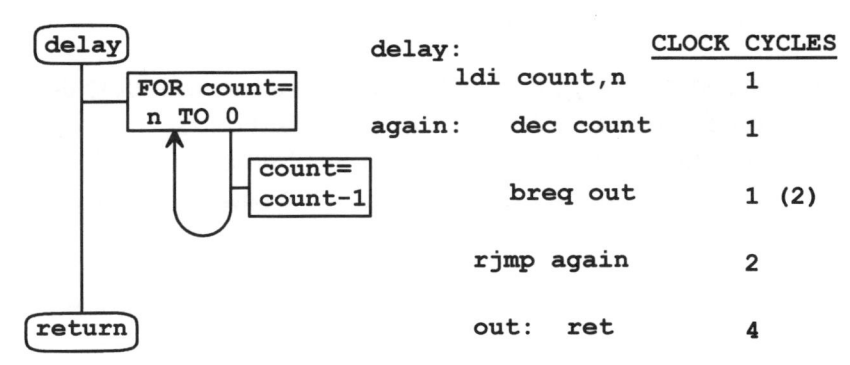

```
                              CLOCK CYCLES
delay:
        ldi count,n             1
again:  dec count               1
        breq out                1 (2)
        rjmp again              2
out:    ret                     4
```

DSD blocks:
- delay
- FOR count= n TO 0
- count = count-1
- return

Note that the DSD loop repeat is always a `rjmp` instruction, and the escape route is always a branch or skip instruction.

This shows up one minor problem with structured programming techniques, the above loop is one line longer than it needs be. The `brne again` instruction could have been used and then the `rjmp` instruction would not have been needed. This does not fit the DSD and you lose the advantages of structuring!

`C' compilers create the same kind of effect, but some can optimise to remove this.

GET GOING WITH . . . AVR MICROCONTROLLERS

You can of course go back over a working program afterwards and optimise the code in this fashion, after the DSD has done it's job.

The subroutine will be called with `rcall delay` and uses only one byte of the stack (no nesting).

We can derive an equation for the time produced by counting the loop cycle instructions in terms of the clock period.
If n is the number in `count` then the delay is :-

delay = 4(n -1) + 6 clock cycles.

This is derived by taking the cycles of the instructions outside the loop adding the extra cycle taken by the branch instruction when it comes out, and then using the number of times round the loop as a multiplier, remembering to take one away because the decrement instruction is done immediately before the test.

This does not include the 3 clock cycles for the `rcall` instruction.

At 1 MHz this gives a maximum delay (with n = $FF) of :-

delay = 4(255 -1) + 6 = 1022 µs or 1.022 ms.

Not long enough! We need more loops, nested inside one another. Let us try two loops.

GET GOING WITH ... AVR MICROCONTROLLERS

The structure now becomes :-

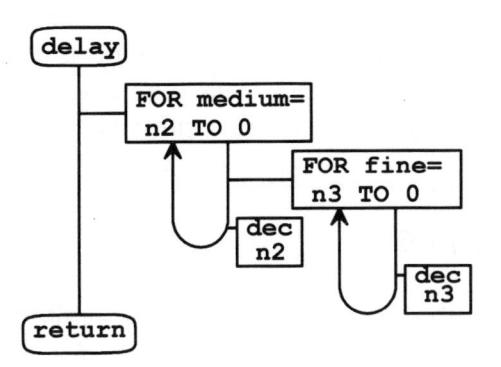

```
delay
 ├── FOR medium=
 │     n2 TO 0
 │     ├── FOR fine=
 │     │     n3 TO 0
 │     ├── dec
 │     │   n2
 │     │       └── dec
 │     │           n3
 return
```

The delay is now the product of the two loops and we should be able to get somewhere near 0.2s by adjusting n2 and n3.

Notice how the DSD shows the nested loops quite nicely.

The structure functions by repeating the fine loop a medium number of times. (Product of the two).

The program is coded as shown below :-

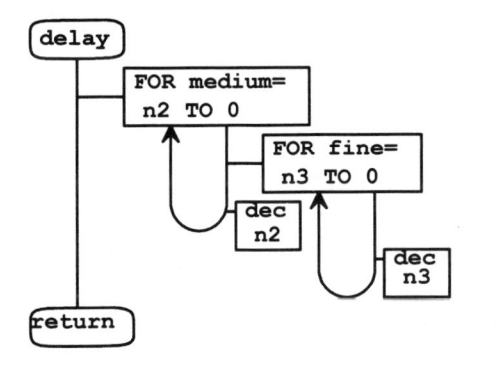

```
delay
 ├── FOR medium=
 │     n2 TO 0
 │     ├── FOR fine=
 │     │     n3 TO 0
 │     ├── dec
 │     │   n2
 │     │       └── dec
 │     │           n3
 return
```

```
delay:
                ldi   medium,n2
magain:         ldi   fine,n3
fagain:         dec   fine
                breq  outf
                rjmp  fagain
outf:           dec   medium
                breq  outm
                rjmp  magain
outm:           ret
```

The code is indented to show the loops. This helps you to follow the program flow.

GET GOING WITH ... AVR MICROCONTROLLERS

The dotted lines are to show how the code loops, which illustrates the nesting concept. This is a good test to do yourself. If the lines cross you have made a mistake! The equation is now a product of the two counters. The odd cycles lost when the branches are taken can usually be ignored simplifying the equation to :-

delay $\approx 4(n2 - 1(n3 - 1)) + 6$

A few simple sums will tell you that the maximum delay available (with n2=n3=255) will be about 258ms. This will do for our purpose. You could adjust it by changing n2 and/or n3. The counter n3 is called fine, because it gives you fine control and n2 is similarly called medium. These will need to be defined at the top of our program, using .def, as with our first program.

Before we try this for real, how about if you wanted a longer delay? Three loops could be used, go on try it your self!
(The coding of this requires careful concentration, put that beer down and give it a try!)

The counters would now be three in quantity, called coarse, medium and fine, because that is the control they would give you. Execution will spend most of its time in the fine loop, occasionally coming out to knock one off the medium or coarse counter and then starting again. For most purposes you can set the fine and medium counters to $FF and adjust the coarse counter to get roughly the delay you need. The labels again should be kept fairly meaningful. The answer is overleaf, see how you got on!

GET GOING WITH ... AVR MICROCONTROLLERS

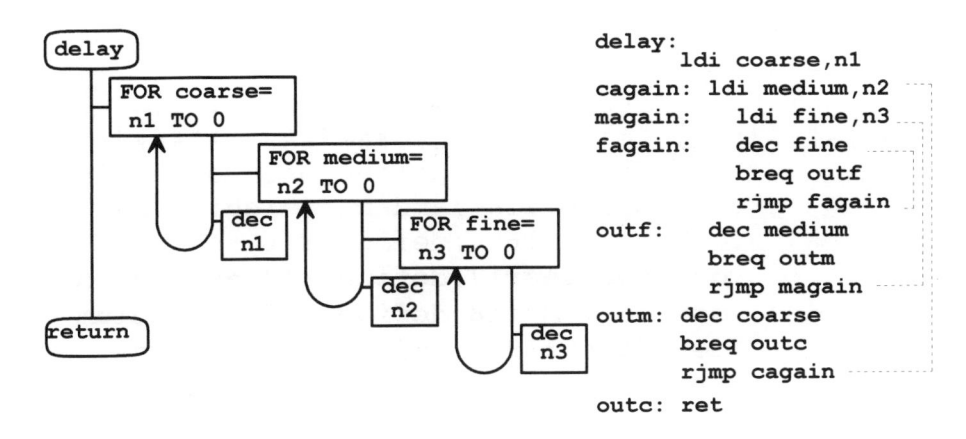

```
delay:
            ldi  coarse,n1
cagain:     ldi  medium,n2
magain:     ldi  fine,n3
fagain:     dec  fine
            breq outf
            rjmp fagain
outf:       dec  medium
            breq outm
            rjmp magain
outm:       dec  coarse
            breq outc
            rjmp cagain
outc:       ret
```

The dotted lines again show how the loops nest inside each other.

The equation now becomes more complex, ignoring the extra cycle taken when the branches are taken, the delay becomes :-

delay ≈ **4(n1 - 1(n2 - 1(n3 - 1))) + 6**   Hard work is'nt it?

The use of the timer/counter is easier to calculate, takes less program memory, but is limited to what 18-bits can give you. Although this can be combined with the above nesting technique to give you as long a delay as you want (seconds-minutes-hours-days - -).

Right, let us write the final version of the program and download to the AVR! The program can be reloaded into the AVR assembler and modified as shown in **bold** overleaf.

GET GOING WITH ... AVR MICROCONTROLLERS

```asm
;##############################################
;#    Example ,program to drive 8 LEDs in a   #
;#    chase pattern.                          #
;#    Target processor AT90S1200              #
;#    Written: Peter Sharpe 25/7/97 Ver. 1.0  #
;##############################################
            .equ ddrb =$17   ;define data direction
            .equ portb=$18   ;and port registers
            .def led =r16    ;define r16 as led
            .def coarse=r17  ;define r17 as coarse
            .def medium=r18  ;define r18 as medium
            .def fine=r19    ;define r19 as fine
            .org $000        ;reset vector in ROM
reset:      rjmp start       ;jump to main program
            .org $004        ;first free ROM space
start:      ser led          ;initialise port B as
            out ddrb,led     ;all outputs
            out portb,led    ;clear LEDs
            clc              ;ensure carry bit=0
ever:       out portb,led    ;write to LEDs
            rol led          ;rotate byte left x1
            rcall delay      ;call delay subroutine
            rjmp ever
;###########Time Delay Subroutine#############
delay:      ldi medium,$FF   ;load medium counter
magain:     ldi fine,$FF     ;load fine counter--
fagain:     dec fine         ;--                |
            breq outf        ;  |               |
            rjmp fagain      ;--                |
outf:       dec medium       ;                  |
            breq outm        ;                  |
            rjmp magain      ;-------------------
outm:       ret              ;returnto main program
```

GET GOING WITH . . . AVR MICROCONTROLLERS

Save the program and assemble it. Now load it into the simulator and try single stepping it again in the same fashion as before. (The set-up should be OK now!) You will soon get tired of clicking the mouse and watching registers decrementing, so run it flat-out, you will see the three registers decrementing at a reasonable speed (depending on the speed of your PC!)!

Now is the time to program the AVR at last. The software will have created a file on the work directory you are using with a .rom extension (chase.rom). This is now loaded into the programmer and the AVR programmed. The routine below describes the process needed for the KANDA starter kit :-

1. *Run Kanda ISP software.*
2. *Select **Project-new project.***
3. *Select AVR 1220 in box and click **OK***
4. *Click in Project Manager window*
5. *Fill in details if you wish, click in any of the three cards to see what is available.*
6. *Click in program memory window.*
7. *Select **File-load** and load in chase.rom.*
8. *Program AVR by **Program-Program Device***
9. *Verify device.*
10. *Unplug AVR (after turning the supply off) and insert in target circuit and switch ON!*

You have now completed your first exercise! Of course it worked first time! (Why not? Mine did.)

GET GOING WITH ... AVR MICROCONTROLLERS

Now let us do the same thing using the timer/counter to generate the time delay.

Chaser program using timer/counter - you can do this two ways, poll the counter or use interrupts. The polling technique would be easier for this application :-

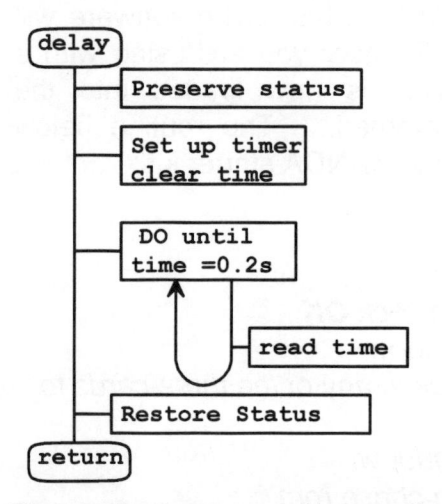

```
delay
  ├── Preserve status
  ├── Set up timer
  │   clear time
  ├── DO until
  │   time =0.2s
  │        ↑
  │        └── read time
  ├── Restore Status
  └── return
```

```
delay:
        in   save,status
        ldi  time,$05
        out  tccr0,time
        clr  time
        out  tcnt0,time
clock:
        in   time,tcnt0
        cpi  time,195
        breq timeout
        rjmp clock
timeout: out status,save
        ret
```

The main program relies on the carry flag, in the status register, to circulate data. The subroutine will affect the flags and hence must preserve this status in a spare register at the start of the subroutine, and then restore it at the end, otherwise the result will be most unexpected (try it!).

We then set the prescalar to clock/1024, giving 1024 μs per count, and clear the counter to zero. The counter then starts incrementing. The loop then repeats, comparing the counter contents with the number of counts needed.

GET GOING WITH ... AVR MICROCONTROLLERS

This is calculated by 0.2 s = 200 ms = 200,000 µs, dividing 200,000 by 1,024 gives us the number to look for in the 8-bit counter tcnt0 (=195). Note the instruction **breq** looks for the Z flag to be set, with the previous compare instruction affecting the flags ready for the branch instruction! If **time=tcnt0** the Z flag is set and the branch is taken.

```
;##############################################
;#      Example 2,program to drive 8 LEDs in a  #
;#      chase pattern, using timer.             #
;#      Target processor AT90S1200              #
;#      Written: Peter Sharpe 25/7/97 Ver. 1.0  #
;##############################################
            .equ ddrb =$17    ;define data direction
            .equ portb=$18    ;and port registers
            .equ tcnt0=$32    ;count contents
            .equ tccr0=$33    ;control register
            .equ status=$3F   ;status register
            .def led =r16     ;define r16 as led
            .def time=r17     ;define r17 as time
            .def save=r18     ;preserve status here
            .org $000         ;reset vector in ROM
reset:      rjmp start        ;jump to main program
            .org $004         ;first free ROM space
;##############################################
start:      ser led           ;initialise port B as
            out ddrb,led      ;all outputs
            out portb,led     ;clear LEDs
            clc               ;ensure carry bit=0
ever:       out portb,led     ;write to LEDs
            rol led           ;rotate byte left x1
            rcall delay       ;call delay subroutine
            rjmp ever
```

GET GOING WITH ... AVR MICROCONTROLLERS

```
;###########Time Delay Subroutine#############
delay:     in save,status    ;preserve status reg.
           ldi time,$05      ;load prescalar
           out tccr0,time    ;via time, clock/1024
           clr time          ;clear counter
           out tcnt0,time    ;via time
clock:     in time,tcnt0     ;read counter
           cpi time,195      ;is it>= 0.2s?
           breq timeout      ;yes, timeout
           rjmp clock        ;no, check again
timeout:   out status,save   ;restore status
           ret               ;returnto main program
```

Reassemble the program as before and load it into the simulator.

Run it this time and look for timer tcnt0 incrementing. You will see this happen every 1024 clocks, indicating that we have set up the pre-scalar tccr0 correctly.

The screenshot shown here is of the register window in the simulator with the program stopped on the 1484th clock cycle. You can see that TCNT has incremented once (at 1024) and r16 (the LED) has the first LED lit.

```
wavrsim
File  View  Window  Breakpoints  Debug  Options  Help

Registers                              _ □ ×
┌Registers──────────┐ ┌Timer 0─────────┐
│ R0  00   R16 FE   │ │ TCCR0    05    │
│ R1  00   R17 01   │ │ TCNT0    01    │
│ R2  00   R18 35   │ │ OCR0     00    │
│ R3  00   R19 00   │ └────────────────┘
│ R4  00   R20 00   │ ┌Special registers┐
│ R5  00   R21 00   │ │        ITHSVNZC │
│ R6  00   R22 00   │ │ SREG  00100001  │
│ R7  00   R23 00   │ │ SP      FFFE    │
│ R8  00   R24 00   │ │ X       0000    │
│ R9  00   R25 00   │ │ Y       0000    │
│ R10 00   R26 00   │ │ Z       0000    │
│ R11 00   R27 00   │ │ PC      14      │
│ R12 00   R28 00   │ │ TIMSK   00      │
│ R13 00   R29 00   │ │ TIFR    00      │
│ R14 00   R30 00   │ │                 │
│ R15 00   R31 00   │ │ CYCLE  001484   │
└───────────────────┘ └─────────────────┘
```

GET GOING WITH . . . AVR MICROCONTROLLERS

The pace is a little slow to see the whole process, so now would be a good time to reprogram the AVR to see if the program does the same job as before.

This is so quick to do, it is worth it just to try it. This would have been impractical with EPROM based MCUs. Incidentally the software, consisting as it does of three separate programmes, is a little unwieldy to run on Windows 3.1, switching from program to program. On WINDOWS 95 it becomes easy to switch between the three tasks. If you have WINDOWS 95 it is probably worth using the AVR STUDIO software, which is more powerful than the simulator. Although it may not control the programmer unless you buy the Atmel version.

Are you impressed so far? Wait till the next chapter!

5   CLEVER STUFF

Now is the time you will want to tackle your own control problems. This will require a variety of techniques, which will need some ingenuity on your part. The instruction set at the rear of this book contains sufficient information to experiment with various instructions, but it is sometimes difficult to `see the wood for the trees'. This chapter attempts to show how some common problems can be solved. It contains complete programmes, and `snippets' of example DSD and code to solve specific types of problem. With such a `rich' instruction set you should be aware that there will always be more than one way of solving a problem. The best solution is the one that works! If this is also the shortest then you have `cracked it'!

LOOK-UP TABLES

These are a collection of data which cannot be described mathematically (and hence calculated). The program may need to access this data either in a sequential manner or a random fashion. Typical applications include driving seven segment displays. The number to display bears no relation to the seven bit number required to achieve the display! Other possible applications include waveform generation, with tables containing frequency and amplitude data.

The table can be stored in EEPROM, where it is permanent, although it can be updated from outside, or internally via program direction.

GET GOING WITH ... AVR MICROCONTROLLERS

The table and diagram below shows the bit pattern and circuit to drive a seven segment display and the actual number displayed.

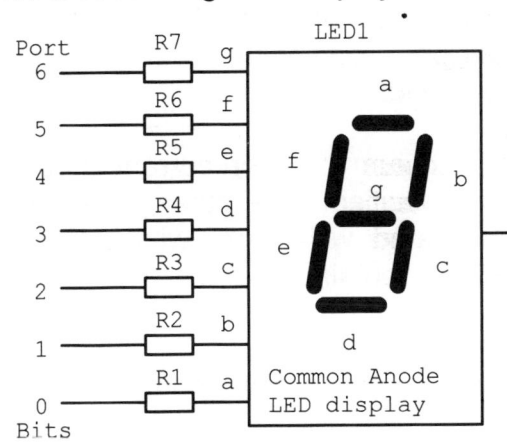

The LED display must be a common anode type, since the ports sink current better than they source.

Current limit resistors R1-R7 should limit the sink current to about 10 mA, 330 Ω is about right for a 5v supply.

No. Seg.	Bit 7	Bit 6 g	Bit 5 f	Bit 4 e	Bit 3 d	Bit 2 c	Bit 1 b	Bit 0 a	HEX No.
0	x	1	0	0	0	0	0	0	$40
1	x	1	1	1	1	0	0	1	$7C
2	x	0	1	0	0	1	0	0	$24
3	x	0	1	1	0	0	0	0	$30
4	x	0	0	1	1	0	0	1	$19
5	x	0	0	1	0	0	1	0	$12
6	x	0	0	0	0	0	1	0	$02
7	x	1	1	1	1	0	0	0	$78
8	x	0	0	0	0	0	0	0	$00
9	x	0	0	1	0	0	0	0	$10

Note that the segment turns on with a logic `0' (current sink) and that there is no relationship between the HEX number at the port to the number displayed on the LED display. There is thus no way of calculating the number prior to sending it out to the port. This screams out for a look-up table.

Beware, we are close to the maximum total port current of 80 mA (70 mA for number 8 display) specified! The other ports, which you may need, must be allocated with care, with total sink currents not exceeding the 10 mA remaining.

The first task is to get the table stored in EEPROM. The assembler will do this for you using a few more assembler directives :-

.ESEG   -   defines the start of an EEPROM segment

.DB   -   defines a constant byte within a program or EEPROM memory

The **.ORG** directive can be used to position the table in EEPROM memory. The few lines of code below show how this would be used:-

```
.eseg
.org $000   ;locates start of table location $000
table:
.db $40,$79,$24,$30,$19,$12,$02,$78,$00,$10
```

It now only remains to find some way to access this table.

GET GOING WITH ... AVR MICROCONTROLLERS

This can easily be done because the EEPROM is separate memory with it's own address range, and we have started our table from $00. So the address equates to the number you want displayed, and the contents of the address is the number required to drive the display. Very convenient.

To access EEPROM is simplicity itself. In the I/O space are three registers controlling access to the EEPROM :-

EECR - is the control register to instigate read or write (strobe).

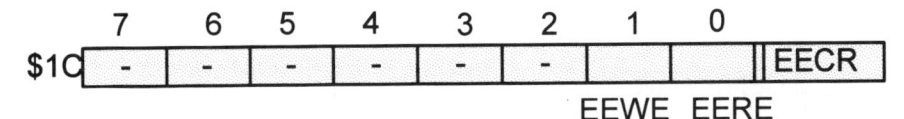

	7	6	5	4	3	2	1	0	
$1C	-	-	-	-	-	-			EECR

                                    EEWE EERE

A `1' in the appropriate bit instigates that action, with the AVR automatically clearing the bit when complete.

EEDR - contains the data to be read or written.

	7	6	5	4	3	2	1	0	
$1D	MSB	-	-	-	-	-	-	LSB	EEDR

EEAR - is the address register for the EEPROM.

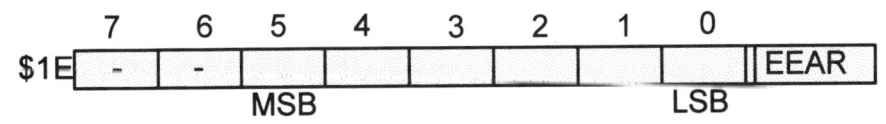

	7	6	5	4	3	2	1	0	
$1E	-	-							EEAR

           MSB   LSB

To read data you set the address to read in EEAR and set the EERE bit in EECR. This triggers a read cycle, with the AVR placing the data in the EEDR register. The EERE bit is cleared automatically by the AVR for the next strobe.

GET GOING WITH ... AVR MICROCONTROLLERS

To write data is slightly more involved, because EEPROM writes take about 2.5 ms. The address is set up in EEAR, the data stored in EEDR and the EEWE bit set in EECR. The program must then poll the EEWE bit until it clears before the next write cycle.

To illustrate the read cycle in action let us contrive a simple program to drive a seven segment display to step through the table to display 0 - 9 with a short delay between. The DSD below shows the structure.

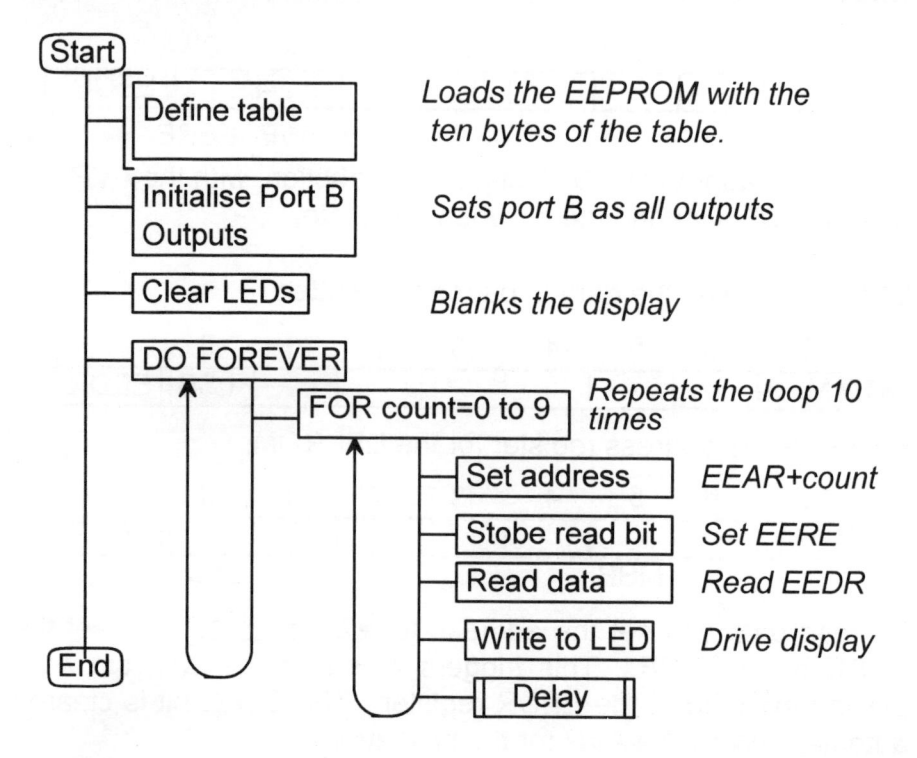

```
Start
 ├─ Define table                Loads the EEPROM with the
 │                              ten bytes of the table.
 ├─ Initialise Port B           Sets port B as all outputs
 │  Outputs
 ├─ Clear LEDs                  Blanks the display
 ├─ DO FOREVER
 │   └─ FOR count=0 to 9        Repeats the loop 10 times
 │       ├─ Set address          EEAR+count
 │       ├─ Stobe read bit      Set EERE
 │       ├─ Read data           Read EEDR
 │       ├─ Write to LED        Drive display
 │       └─ Delay
End
```

GET GOING WITH ... AVR MICROCONTROLLERS

```
;##################################################
;#      Example program to drive 7-segment        #
;#      display in 0 -9 count in one second steps #
;#      Target processor AT90S1200                #
;#      Written: Peter Sharpe 25/7/97 Ver. 1.0    #
;##################################################
        .equ ddrb =$17         ;define data direction
        .equ portb=$18         ;and port registers
        .equ tcnt0=$32         ;timer value
        .equ tccr0=$33         ;timer control
        .equ status=$3F        ;status register
        .equ eear=$1E          ;EEPROM address
        .equ eedr=$1D          ;data and
        .equ eecr=$1C          ;control registers
        .def count=r16         ;led number is here
        .def time=r17          ;time is here
        .def save=r18          ;preserve status etc., here
        .org $000              ;reset vector

        rjmp start             ;jump to main program
        .org $004              ;first free space
start:  ser count              ;initialise port B as
        out ddrb,count         ;all outputs
        out portb,count        ;blank LED segments
ever:   clr count              ;clear FOR loop counter
for:        out eear,count
            sbi eecr,0         ;read eeprom at count
            in save,eedr
            out portb,save     ;send to led

            rcall delay        ;wait 0.2 s

            inc count
            cpi count,10       ;is it no. 9?
                breq out       ;yes, come out
            rjmp for           ;no, do again
out:    rjmp ever
```

119

GET GOING WITH ... AVR MICROCONTROLLERS

```
;###############Time Delay####################
delay:      in save,status      ;preserve status reg
            ldi time,$05        ;load prescalar
            out tccr0,time      ;via time, clock/1024
            clr time            ;clear counter

            out tcnt0,time      ;via time
clock:         in time,tcnt0    ;read timer
               cpi time,255     ;is it = 0.2s?
               breq timeout     ;yes, timeout
               rjmp clock       ;no, check again
timeout:    out status,save     ;restore status
            ret                 ;return to main program

;###############table########################
            .eseg
            .org 0
table:      .db $40,$7c,$24,$30,$19,$12,$02,$78,$00,$10
```

The delay routine is from the previous example and gives about 0.2s delay on a 1MHz clock.

The .eseg directive tells the assembler to generate another file containing the bytes after the .db directive. This will have the same file name but a different file extension (.eep).

To program the AVR we would now have to load in two files to the programmer, the .rom version into program memory and the .eep version into EEPROM. The programmer also programmes the AVR independently so you will need to program the AVR twice, one for the program and one for the EEPROM.

ASSEMBLER UPDATE

You may have noticed that the programmes are starting to get cluttered with equates and symbol definitions. Most of which are contained in every program you write! As you get more addicted to the AVR range you will also want to play with other variants with more facilities. You soon lose track of which instructions are available on each variant! Try writing to static ram on the AVR 1200! (It has none!)

The assembler caters for both of these by allowing you directives to cope :-

.include "<file>" - inserts this file into the source code at assembly time. This is an ideal place to put all the normal equates for the device in use.

.device <type no.> - tells the assembler which variant you
  (AT90S1200) are using and checks that the
  (AT90S2313) instructions you use in the source file
  (AT90S4414) are valid for it. If you make a mistake
  (AT90S8515) it will tell you!

Atmel even provide include files for each variant with their software. You do not even have to write them!

The rest of the examples will use these methods to show how it is done. *(Warning! My version of the assembler called the 1200, 1300 - an early version I think!)*

ANALOGUE WORK

The AVRs all have one comparator built-in, all-be-it on different port pins (very confusing-why Atmel?) which allow analogue sensing to be achieved. This may seem rather limiting compared to some of the big PICs, for instance, which have up to 8 analogue input channels, with a proper Analogue to Digital Converter (ADC). At first glance this may seem true but availability of fast, cheap, and small serial (SPI) ADCs are now so good, and they outperform the in-built PIC ADCs, that this makes it uneconomical. The extra cost of including the circuitry on-chip for the occasional use does not make it viable. If you need full blown ADC then use one of the many serial ADCs on the market (e.g. MAXIM MAX 1110/1111).

The comparator idea is cheap and surprisingingly useful, and allows simple level sensing. If you need ADC then this can be obtained with Pulse Width Modulation (PWM) or DAC techniques to provide reasonable accuracy ADC.

PWM provides a binary digital output waveform whose period is constant but whose duty cycle (delta δ) is changed.

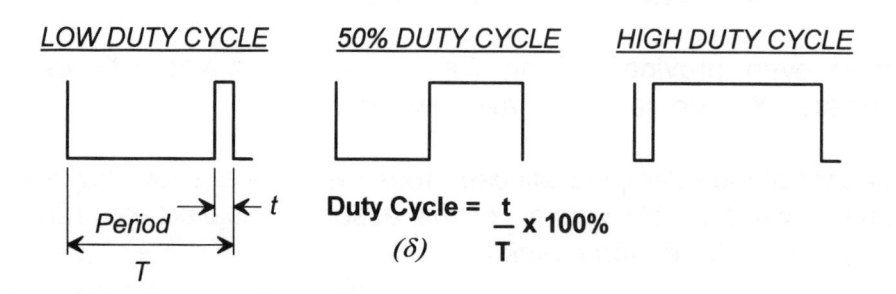

LOW DUTY CYCLE   *50% DUTY CYCLE*   *HIGH DUTY CYCLE*

Period T, pulse width t

$$\text{Duty Cycle} = \frac{t}{T} \times 100\% \quad (\delta)$$

GET GOING WITH . . . AVR MICROCONTROLLERS

This is easily generated in software and the larger AVRs have special circuitry to make it very easy to produce.

Why, I hear you ask? Well, if you average this waveform out, either with a filter circuit, or by an inductive load (such as a motor) you will discover that you get a average voltage which is directly proportional to the duty cycle. On a motor this provides efficient speed control. On a 5v supply this gives you analogue output voltages (after filtering) of about :-

Duty Cycle %	0	10	20	30	40	50	60	70	80	90	100
Mean value (V)	0	0.5	1.0	1.5	2.0	2.5	3.0	3.5	4.0	4.5	5.0

The simple filter circuit shown below can be employed, connected to an output pin producing the PWM pattern.

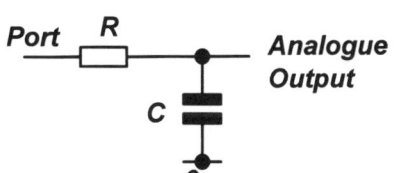

The values of R and C are chosen to suit the load placed on the output and the frequency of the waveform.

To make the AVR provide an ADC you can use this output as the voltage reference to one of the comparator inputs, produce a ramp or triangular waveform at the port by incrementing the duty cycle over a period of time and sense the point at which the two are equal.

GET GOING WITH . . . AVR MICROCONTROLLERS

The digital value to produce the PWM value at that point is now proportional to the analogue input voltage. This is the same principle as used in the cheaper ADCs chips on the market.

One application of this method is motor speed control.
The simple example shown below using the AVR 1200, provides for variable speed control of a cheap DC motor. (Model trains etc.,)

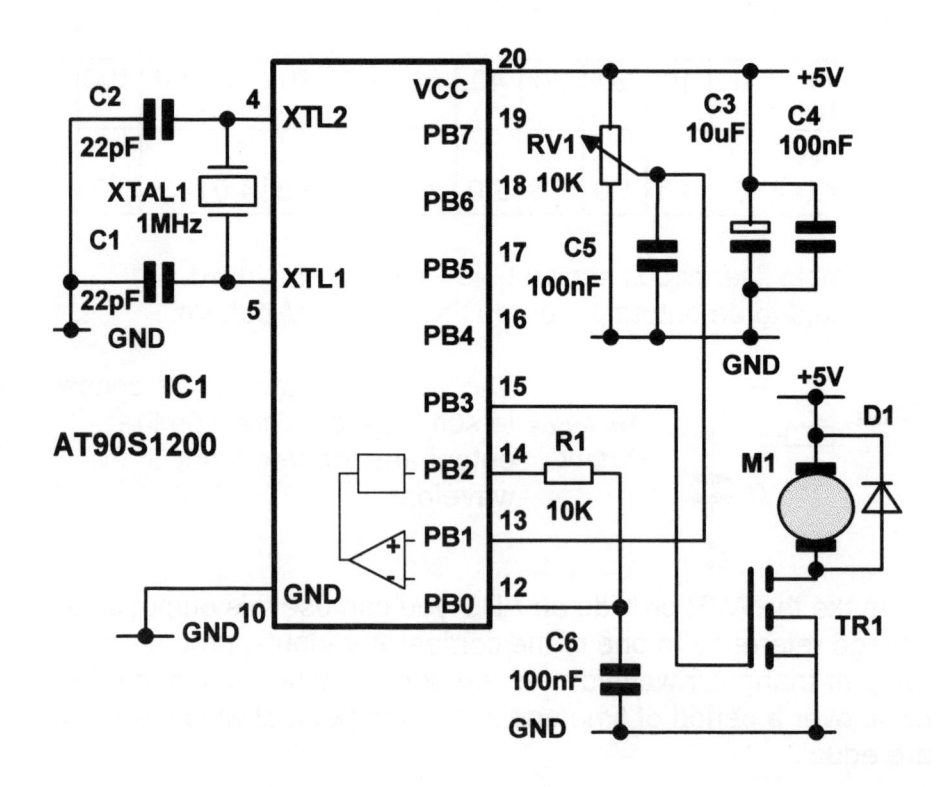

GET GOING WITH . . . AVR MICROCONTROLLERS

The motor is driven from a power MOSFET (VN46, IRF530 etc.,), with fast diode D1 (1N4148) protecting the transistor from the back emf of the motor.

Variable resistor RV1 provides a variable potential divider giving an adjustable output voltage of 0 - 5v. The capacitor C5 removes any potential noise produced by the wiper of RV1. If the value is increased it could also act as inertia simulation for such things as model trains.

Resistor R1 and capacitor C5 filter the PWM output, which will appear from port PB2, into a triangular waveform, generated by the program. This analogue voltage is compared with the voltage from RV1 and used to control the PWM produced at port PB3 to drive the motor via TR1.

This form of control is very efficient, producing very few losses.

The program required for this must use interrupts, since the job of the main program will be to generate the triangular waveform, turning the motor on at the start of the cycle. The interrupt service routine will be triggered when the analogue comparator changes and will need to turn the motor off.

It would take little extra work to monitor the back-emf of the motor and use it to provide speed feedback, keeping the speed constant despite load changes. (Closed Loop Control - Servo). This would require an extra bit to disable the back-emf monitoring until the off period.

GET GOING WITH ... AVR MICROCONTROLLERS

The only problem with this arrangement is that the AT90S1200 has no hardware support for PWM generation. The PWM pattern would need to be done in software. This can be done but produces a low frequency pattern from a 1MHz clock (a few hundred Hz). This method is thus more suited to the larger AVRs with PWM generation hardware, or you could use a higher frequency clock.

The other method uses a few output bits to produce the triangular waveform by DAC techniques. Digital to Analogue Converters (DACs) count up in binary with each output driving a resistor arrangement, with values either in the weighting 1-2-4-8 etc., or using the R-2R ladder network. Both of these produce an analogue voltage proportional to the binary number put in. Four bits would give us SIXTEEN steps (2^4=16) in our ramp, which when filtered produces a reasonable linear ramp when fed from a digital count. The diagram below shows how this is achieved :-

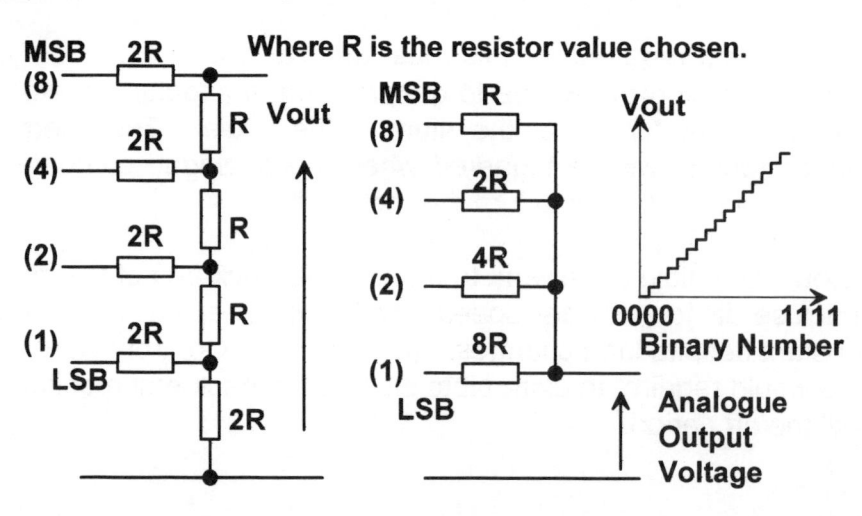

GET GOING WITH . . . AVR MICROCONTROLLERS

The R-2R method is usually used, although it employs more resistors, because of the easy values, making it suitable for 8, or more bit conversion. The 1-2-4-8- method produces awkward value resistors, limiting the circuit to a few bits. For four bits though it becomes easy, especially if you use a little imagination! The circuit below uses this technique to produce the ramp waveform for comparison:-

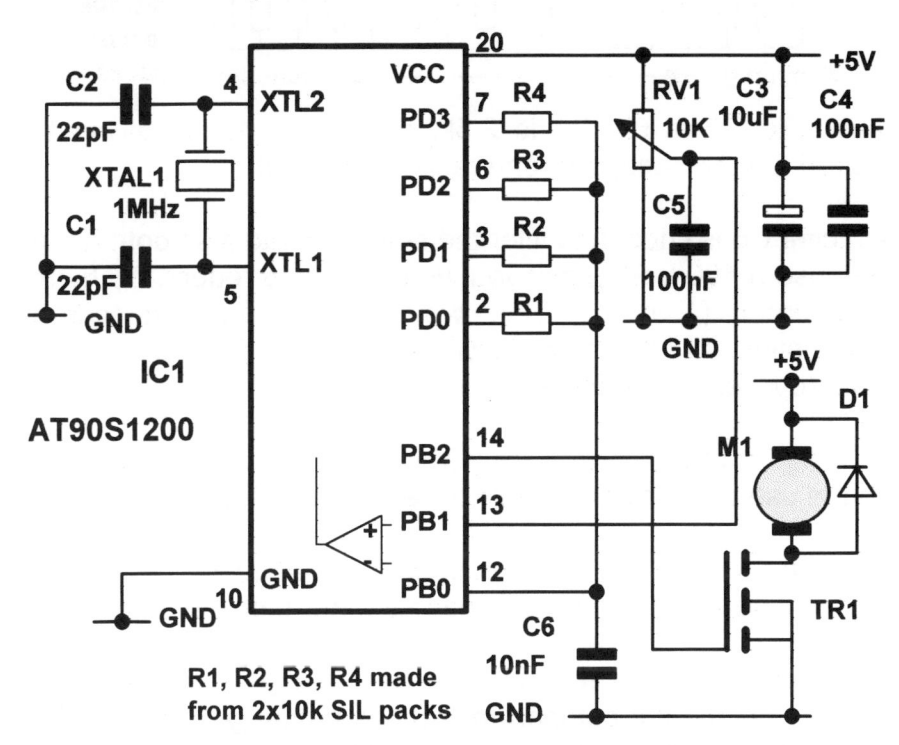

R1, R2, R3, R4 made from 2x10k SIL packs

The bottom four bits of port D are used to produce the binary count (makes the program easier 0-15). The motor is now driven from bit 2 of port B via the power MOSFET.

GET GOING WITH . . . AVR MICROCONTROLLERS

The 1-2-4-8 resistor value is difficult to produce with preferred values but easy to make with the small octal SIL resistor packs. Two packs can be connected thus :-

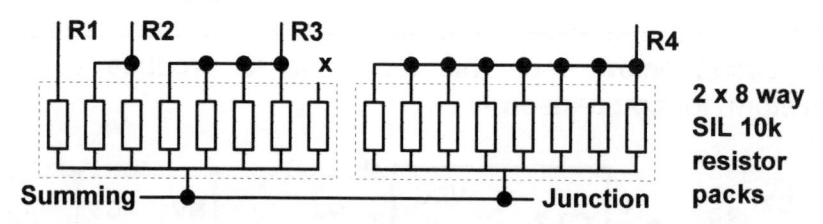

```
     R1   R2      R3                          R4
                                                    2 x 8 way
                                                    SIL 10k
                                                    resistor
     Summing                         Junction       packs
```

R1 is 10k, R2 is 5k, R3 is 2.5k, and R4 is 1.25k, giving the required 8-4-2-1 ratio, with one resistor unused!

Capacitor C6 is chosen to filter the staircase into a smooth ramp. If you use a 100 k SIL pack you would need to reduce C6 by the same order (1 nF). This would make for less current consumption, and this should always be a consideration.
(*I had 10 k versions handy!*)

Let us try to write the software (firmware). This is best achieved with the use of interrupts, in this case the comparator.

The main program needs to produce the triangular waveform by incrementing and then decrementing the low nibble of port D.

The Interrupt service routine only has to toggle the motor bit on/off every time the comparator senses a change in state. This will occur when the speed demand voltage from RV1 equals the ramp voltage produced by the 1-2-4-8 resistor circuit.

GET GOING WITH . . . AVR MICROCONTROLLERS

The end result will be a PWM switching pattern on the gate of the MOSFET, producing speed control of the motor.

<u>Design Stucture Diagram for the Main program.</u>

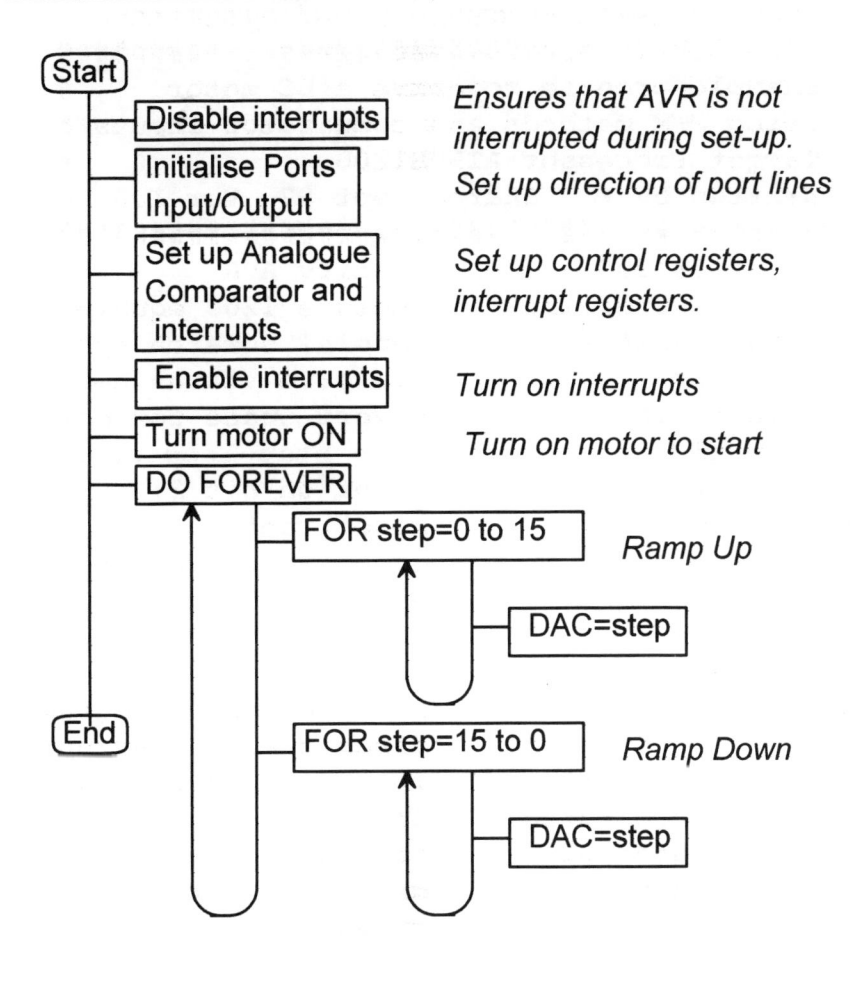

```
Start
 ├─ Disable interrupts              Ensures that AVR is not
 │                                  interrupted during set-up.
 ├─ Initialise Ports
 │  Input/Output                    Set up direction of port lines
 │
 ├─ Set up Analogue                 Set up control registers,
 │  Comparator and                  interrupt registers.
 │  interrupts
 │
 ├─ Enable interrupts               Turn on interrupts
 │
 ├─ Turn motor ON                   Turn on motor to start
 ├─ DO FOREVER
 │      ├─ FOR step=0 to 15         Ramp Up
 │      │      └─ DAC=step
 │      │
 │      └─ FOR step=15 to 0         Ramp Down
 │             └─ DAC=step
End
```

GET GOING WITH... AVR MICROCONTROLLERS

The main program can now be coded, using our new method of include files and device type checking. Pay particular attention to how the interrupts are controlled and the vectors set. The first line of the program (main) must disable interrupts (cli) until all the ports are initialised, and interrupt control registers set:-

```
;################################################
;#      Example program to drive a DC motor     #
;#      using PWM methods and comparator inputs #
;#      Target Processor AT90S1200              #
;#      Written by P J Sharpe Sept 97  Ver 1.0  #
;################################################
.device at90s1200           ;specify AVR
.include "1200def.inc"      ;include 1200 equates
.def scratch=r16            ;general scratch space
.def save=r17               ;preserve status here
.def invert=r18             ;invert space for eor
.def step=r19               ;ramp step loop counter
.equ motor=2                ;motor on bit 2
.org $000                   ;reset vector
     rjmp main              ;go to main program
     nop                    ;ext. int. not used
     nop                    ;timer int.not used
     rjmp adc               ;comparator   interrupt
main:                       ;start of main program
     cli                    ;disable all interrupts
     ldi scratch,$fc        ;initialise port b as
     out ddrb,scratch       ;I/O port
     ldi scratch,$ff        ;initialise portd for
     out ddrd,scratch       ;dac 1-2-4-8 resistor
                            ;drive
```

GET GOING WITH ... AVR MICROCONTROLLERS

```
          clr scratch              ;set comparator mode
          out acsr,scratch         ;to interrupt on change
          ldi invert,$04           ;initialise eor mask
          sei                      ;enable all interrupts
          sbi acsr,acie            ;enable comparator int.
          sbi portb,motor          ;turn motor on to start
do:       clr step                 ;set dac to bottom step
up:       out portd,step           ;dac step up
          inc step                 ;step = step +1
          cpi step,16              ;is it top step?
          breq next                ;yes ? Go to step down
          rjmp up                  ;no step up again
next:     ldi step,15              ;set dac to top step
          out portd,step           ;dac step down
          dec step                 ;step = step - 1
          breq out                 :is it bottom step?
          rjmp down                ;no step down again
out:      rjmp do                  ;ramp again
```

Note: Because of the way the AVR instructions operate some registers have had to be used for manipulation. Inversion on one bit is done with the EOR instruction. Excusive ORing the motor bit only, inverts it each time round the loop. The AVR requires this done in a register, so `invert` has been used for this purpose. The step counter `step` is used to count between 0 and 15.

Between the disabling and enabling of global interrupts the ports have been initialised and the comparator interrupt mode set and enabled. A general purpose register `scratch` has been allocated for accumulator type storage.

GET GOING WITH ... AVR MICROCONTROLLERS

The interrupt service routine has a simple job to do, just toggle the motor on/off:-

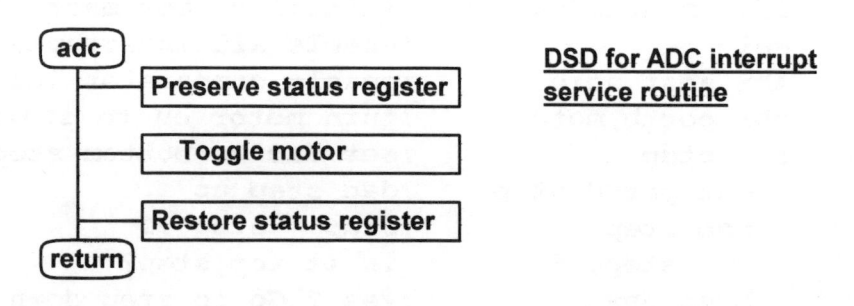

```
adc
 ├── Preserve status register
 ├── Toggle motor
 └── Restore status register
return
```

DSD for ADC interrupt service routine

```
;##################################################
;Comparator interrupt service routine to toggle
;motor bit
;##################################################

adc:    in   save,sreg           ;preserve status reg.
        in   scratch,portb       ;read motor bit
        eor  scratch,invert      ;invert it to toggle
        out  portb,scratch       ;and write it out again
        out  sreg,save           ;restore status reg.
        reti                     ;return to main prog.
```

<u>NOTES</u>:   The toggling is done by EOR the data at port B with a `1' in the motor bit position. (Invert was set to $04=value of bit 2, where the motor is!)   Only this bit is then inverted, with all other bits left alone. A very useful technique.

GET GOING WITH . . . AVR MICROCONTROLLERS

This program can be typed in and assembled as before. The simulation poses a few problems. It is easy to check that the main loop is working, but how do you check the interrupt? Well on this simulator you cannot (poor show what, give software away and only do half a job!). This is another reason why people pay big money for ICE systems! There are better simulators on the market that show the ports and allow interrupts to be simulated. AVR STUDIO is better at this kind of work, but you need WINDOWS 95!

The best way is to try it out on the AVR. If you have an oscilloscope then you can monitor the waveforms at various duty cycles.

Expected waveform on PB0 (Triangular RAMP):-

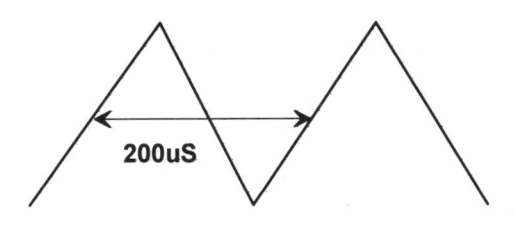

200uS

Expected waveforms on gate of MOSFET at various Duty Cycles:-

LOW DUTY CYCLE	50% DUTY CYCLE	HIGH DUTY CYCLE
	200uS	
RV1 near 0v	RV1 halfway	RV1 near 5v
LOW SPEED	**MEDIUM SPEED**	**HIGH SPEED**

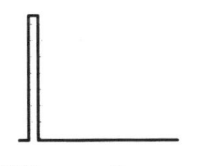

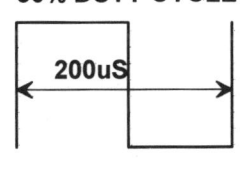

GET GOING WITH . . . AVR MICROCONTROLLERS

WATCH DOG TIMER (WDT)

The previous example is controlling a device which generates a lot of interference. Small DC motors, certainly the cheap one I used, produce vast amounts of noise from the brushes and commutator segments, as they switch. This can corrupt any MCU and cause the firmware to `crash'. We could use the previous example to show how the watch dog timer can recover from any crash, enabling the MCU to reset and regain control.

The WDT is controlled by one register in I/O space called WDTCR ($21). The first three bits set the prescalar option from an internal 1MHz clock and the fourth bit turns on the WDT. All we need to do is to add the WDT set up instructions at the start of the program and ensure that we clear the WDT somewhere round the main loop. The main loop takes about 0.2ms (about 5KHz PWM) so we need to reset the WDT during this period. Alternatively we could get closer protection if we put the WDT timer reset in the step up and step down loop itself. This repeats every 5υs or so. To ensure normal operation we must place the WDT reset instruction with care. In this case it could go at the bottom of the main loop, with the prescalar set to a time greater than the 0.2 ms taken around the loop.

The WDT prescalar could be set to 256 cycles giving a reset time of 0.256 ms (WDT runs at 1MHz, so 256 x 1 μs = 256 μs).
This gives a bit of spare time to allow for tolerances in the frequency.

GET GOING WITH ... AVR MICROCONTROLLERS

The structure now becomes :-

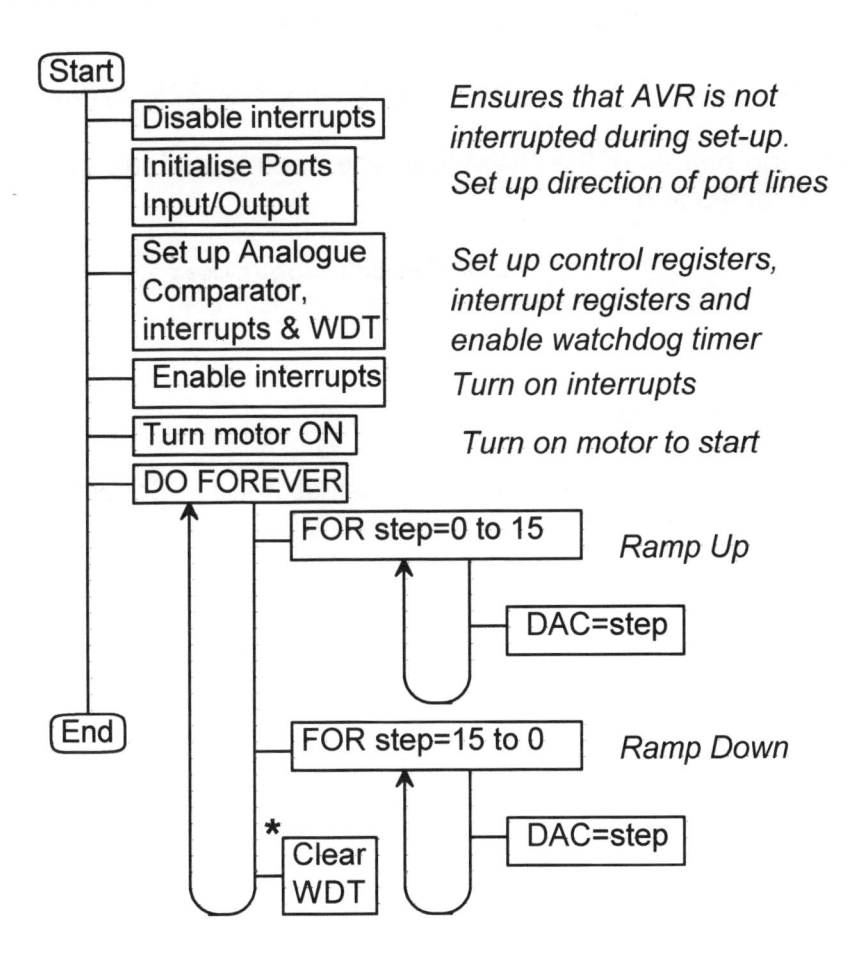

```
Start
 ├─ Disable interrupts          Ensures that AVR is not
 │                              interrupted during set-up.
 ├─ Initialise Ports
 │  Input/Output                Set up direction of port lines
 │
 ├─ Set up Analogue             Set up control registers,
 │  Comparator,                 interrupt registers and
 │  interrupts & WDT            enable watchdog timer
 │
 ├─ Enable interrupts           Turn on interrupts
 │
 ├─ Turn motor ON               Turn on motor to start
 │
 ├─ DO FOREVER
 │     ├─ FOR step=0 to 15      Ramp Up
 │     │     └─ DAC=step
 │     │
 │     ├─ FOR step=15 to 0      Ramp Down
 │     │     └─ DAC=step
 │     │
 │     * Clear
 │       WDT
End
```

* indicates where we need a WDR instruction.

The interrupt routine remains unchanged.

GET GOING WITH ... AVR MICROCONTROLLERS

The following line needs to be added at the top of the program (anywhere between the cli and sei instructions) :-

```
ldi wdtcr,$c0    ;enable WDT and set 256 cycles
```

Towards the bottom of the PWM loop you need to add the watch dog reset instruction :-

```
     wdr              ;clear watch dog timer
```

e.g.

```
out: wdr         ;clear WDT
     rjmp do
```

The program is now fully protected against noise. Should the program crash, the WDT will reset the MCU and the control program will reboot, regaining control.

6 POTENTIAL CLEVER STUFF

If you intend to make a habit of programming MCUs it might pay you to consider other, more refined, methods. There are two ways you can improve matters :-

ICE - In Circuit Emulation, allows you to download the program to a piece of hardware pretending to be a MCU, and provides accurate feedback of performance, either at full speed, or by single stepping. This saves you downloading the program to the AVR until you are certain it works to specification. AVR STUDIO works with the Atmel ICE automatically and also with the IAR `C' software discussed next.

The Atmel I.C.E system

GET GOING WITH... AVR MICROCONTROLLERS

Other ICE systems are appearing on the market which may be cheaper. KANDA Systems is another useful contact. This company is developing an ICE system for the AVR and it should be available by the time you read this!

PROGRAM IN `C' - the language of the professional software engineer, and the one the AVR was designed for.

PROGRAMMING IN `C'

This is an acquired skill - not everyone takes to `C', although software engineers love it. The language is not so obvious as, say, BASIC, or other languages you may have tried. It does provide efficient code compilation from a medium level language to pure object code. This is especially true of the AVR which was designed to be programmed in `C'!

The `C' compiler was designed first and then the instruction set designed from this. Code conversion is thus very efficient, something that cannot be said for other MCUs like the PIC, which can also be programmed in `C'.

This is not a cheap alternative! The software is fairly expensive but will pay for itself if you are doing this for a living.

I use the `C' development software from IAR Systems. This is a professional development suite containing all the tools you need to develop and refine programmes for a range of MCUs. This compiler was developed in conjunction with Atmel, and in parallel with the design of the AVR.

GET GOING WITH ... AVR MICROCONTROLLERS

It can also support most other MCUs, but you are unlikely to achieve such an efficient code conversion. A demo version of the IAR WORKBENCH is available on CD-ROM and is well worth a play! A support book is also available written by a `well known' author (I hope)!!

The IAR software provides :-

WORKBENCH

An integrated control shell providing access to all the other tools. A very powerful editor is included which highlights and formats the source code automatically for you. This automatically indents the loops and highlights the structures to make the program more readable. It also allows simple access to the huge facilities provided by this powerful suite of software.
Various windows can be opened so that you can keep an eye on progress. If run on WINDOWS 95 you can even multitask so that compilation is taking place while you are typing the next program, or printing the previous one!

C - COMPILER

Takes the `C' source code from the editor and compiles it into object code. The compiler can be set up to provide various levels of optimisation. The code produced can be optimised for speed, or memory space, or a mixture of both. This goes through the code and rearranges it to remove such things as the extra lines caused by structuring, encountered earlier, or selects other instructions to improve speed.

GET GOING WITH . . . AVR MICROCONTROLLERS

This is possible with the AVR because it has a very rich instruction set and there is always more than one way of doing things. The optimiser chooses the best to suit your requirements. To do this manually would take a long time, and a lot of experience. The end result is executable code that is very compact and efficient.

ASSEMBLER

Allows the code generated to be modified or inspected. You can even use it to program the AVR. It is very much more powerful than the Atmel version. You can use this to refine the code produced by the compiler, if you can improve on the optimiser!

LINKER

Allows program code to be built from a variety of code segments from libraries and your compiled source code. It links library files with your original source code to produce the final program.

LIBRARIAN

Handles the making and using of useful routines which can be included in your programmes that need them. In time you can save a considerable amount of development work by making your programmes from unique code linked with libraries of useful functions that you have built up over a period of time.

GET GOING WITH ... AVR MICROCONTROLLERS

DEBUGGER (C-SPY)

Allows you to single step, set breakpoints and other debugging techniques, on C source code as well as assembly language. Very useful! It traces the values of variables in a watch window so that you can check your program is functioning.

If you want to experiment with this powerful suite of software, IAR provide a demo CD (address provided in the appendix) which provides a fully working version. The only thing you cannot do is supply OUTPUT! (*If you have a sound board it does play some nice music for you though!*)

Various training courses are provided using this software. These are not cheap but they provide a rapid entry to the methods and will pay for themselves quickly if you use the system professionally. KANDA systems (address at rear), in conjunction with the MCU Training unit at Chippenham College run a 5-day residential course using AVRs with IAR `C' software.

KANDA act as booking agents and provide hardware and software support. Software and hardware are available to buy at a reduced price from such courses, and some even give kit away!

The KANDA/Chippenham College course provides books/data sheets/CD ROMS and AVR Starter Kits, along with very comfortable `live-in' training, first class accomodation and food, in an `olde worlde' hotel on the edge of the Cotswolds. The site was carefully chosen to be on the M4 corridor/Railway link to Heathrow airport.

FAREWELL

That's All Folks! I hope you enjoyed the read and found the book useful. My various projects encountered over the next few months development work will eventually appear in an AVR Cookbook. These should prove useful to students at HNC/HND or Degree level because they are my Guinea Pigs!

APPENDIX A

GLOSSARY

(Some terms commonly found in Micro-Based Systems)

ADC Analogue to Digital Converter - a circuit converting varying signals to binary digital data.

ADDRESS BUS Wires or tracks carrying the address of a memory location from the micro to memory.

ADDRESS DECODER Circuit switching between blocks of memory, ensuring that only one device 'talks' at a time.

ALU Arithmetic and Logic Unit - the processing part of the microcontroller.

ANALOGUE A term which covers systems and devices which handle electrical signals that vary continuously with time.

ASSEMBLY LANGUAGE A simple collection of Mnemonics used to represent more complicated machine code instructions. Source code written in this can be compiled by simple assemblers to produce one-to-one conversion object code. The most efficient programming language, but can be difficult to follow.

ASYNC-HRONOUS Data communicated without any timing information, relying on precise timing of devices.

APPENDIX A

AVR Alf (Bogen) Vergard (Wollan) Risc microcontroller from Atmel Norway design team.

BCD Binary Coded Decimal, the binary range covered by four bits but limited to the digits 0 - 9, allowing simple conversion to decimal devices such as displays. (NOT a true number system.)

BINARY A number system using only two numbers `0' and `1', suited to digital logic circuits.

BIT Binary digIT, one logic level represented by a voltage level, `1' normally near the supply rail e.g. +5v, `0' near the 0v rail.

BUS A collection of wires or tracks on a printed circuit board.

BUS CONFLICT Two or more devices attempting to talk at the same time on the same bus. A result of faulty hardware design (address decoding) and results in data corruption or hardware failure.

BYTE Eight bits in parallel.

C A high level portable language producing efficient code when compiled into machine code.

APPENDIX A

CARRY — A bit created by an overflow from the normal word size, e.g the ninth bit of an eight bit number.

CHIP — See IC.

CISC — Complex Instruction Set Computer - a computer having a large instruction set capable of most things but resulting in slower execution times.

CS — Chip Select, a control line enabling a chip to work.

CLEAR — A logic `0' created by some action.

COMPILER — A software application taking a high level language source file and creating a machine code object file capable of running on the target processor.

DAC — Digital to Analogue Converter - a circuit to convert binary digital data to varying electrical signals.

DATA BUS — Wires or tracks carrying data to or from the micro.

DIGITAL — A term which covers systems and devices which handle electrical signals that vary discontinuously with time (steps), usually binary 0 and 1.

DSD — Design Structure Diagram, a modified form of flowchart showing program flow in a diagrammatic fashion and forcing a structured approach.

APPENDIX A

DOUBLE WORD	A thirty-two bit number (2 x 16).
DRAM	Dynamic RAM. Memory made from capacitor cells (Gate-Source capacitance of MOSFET) requiring refreshing every few milli-seconds as the charge leaks away. Four times smaller than SRAM, but slower to access. Available in much larger sizes but difficult to use as a refresh controller is required.
EEPROM	Electrically Erasable Programmable Read Only Memory. A non-volatile ROM programmed by normal voltage levels and erased by normal voltage levels (usually). Normally slow to program, but can be reused many times.
EPROM	Erasable Programmable Read Only Memory. A non-volatile ROM programmed by higher voltage levels than normal and erased by exposure to Ultra-Violet light. Most expensive ROM, but can be reused many times.
FIRMWARE	Programmes stored in ROM, usually the operating system.
FLAG	An individual bit in a register indicating or controlling some event.
FLASH	A type of non-volatile memory ROM capable of fast read and write, usually at normal supply levels.

APPENDIX A

HARDWARE The components of a system. (Electronic and Mechanical).

HARVARD Computer architecture having separate address buses for memory devices, a wider word size for program memory, allowing single line programmes.

HEXA-DECIMAL A number system to a base of 16, useful for work with binary digital systems and having sixteen digits, 0, 1, 2, 3, 4, 5, 6, 7, 8, 9, A, B, C, D, E, F representing four bits from 0000 to 1111.

IC Integrated Circuit (CHIP), containing many electronic components to form a circuit, made on a silicon subtrate.

I²C Inter- IC connection system, providing serial communication protocols for medium speed transmission and reception between ICs.

INTERFACE Connection point of peripheral devices to/from a micro-based system.

INTERRUPT The action of a micro stopping execution of the main program and switching to another on instigation of a signal from elsewhere. (Hardware or Software.)

ISP In System Programming - the ability of a device to be programmed in circuit without disconnection.

APPENDIX A

MACHINE CODE The language of the processor, a binary code representing some instruction to the MPU.

MNEMONIC An `aid to memory', a series of letters used as short-hand to represent longer instructions.
e.g SEC means **SE**t the **C**arry Flag.

MPU Micro Processor Unit. A digital circuit to provide programmable logic functions, requiring other support ICs.

MCU Micro Controller Unit, a complete micro-based system on a single chip.

NIBBLE Four bits.

NON - VOLATILE Refers to memory devices which DO NOT lose their contents when power is removed.

OBJECT CODE Machine code created by a compiler to run on a processor.

OCTAL A number system to a base of 8, having eight digits, 0 to 7 and representing three bits from 000 to 111. Useful for micro-based systems working with word sizes in multiples of three.

OP-CODE Operation Code - the machine code instruction.

OPERAND The data used by the Op-Code.

APPENDIX A

PARALLEL Many bits of information together to make a complete data word.

PERIPHERAL A device connected to the outside of a system.

RAM Random Access Memory. Read and write memory usually volatile in nature.

READ Data travelling into the micro.

REGISTER A storage location inside a device, usually a micro. or support IC.

RESET A means of starting a micro from the beginning or clearing a bit to `0'.

RISC Reduced Instruction Set Computer - having a smaller but hardware efficient instruction set. Most commonly used instructions are provided, others are made from those available. Fast execution time.

ROM Read Only Memory. A non-volatile memory programmed at manufacture by an aluminium mask.
Expensive one-off costs but cheapest type in large quantities.

SERIAL Data sent or received ONE bit at a time.

APPENDIX A

SET A logic `1' created by some action.

SINK Current flow into the output of a device (from supply), usually at logic `0' state.

SOFTWARE Programmes stored in RAM.

SOURCE Current flow out of a device (to 0v), usually at logic`1' state.

SOURCE CODE A text file containing assembly language and comments as input to assemblers or compilers, for translation to object code.

SPI Serial Peripheral Interface - a method of sending and receiving fast data in serial form between two or more devices.

SRAM Static RAM made from bistable cells (Flip-flops). Fastest type of RAM and easy to use, but larger than DRAM on chip, taking four times the chip area.

STATUS Status Register, a location inside a micro, recording events occurring during program execution in individual bits called FLAGs, and controlling various actions of the micro.

APPENDIX A

SYNC-HRONOUS Data communication having timing information included to synchronise transmission and reception speeds.

TRI-STATE Micro devices have three states, `0', `1' and `Z', high impedance or OFF. This allows other devices to take control of the same bus without conflict.

VOLATILE Refers to memory devices which lose their contents when power is removed.

VON NEUMANN The original architecture of microprocessors having a common address bus for all memory devices.

WORD Either a sixteen bit number, or the number of bits used by the system for data, depending on context.

WRITE Data travelling out of the micro.

APPENDIX B

AVR DATA SUMMARY

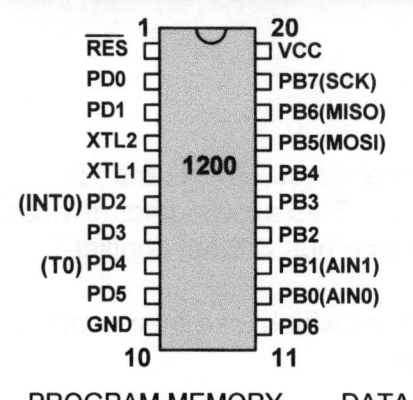

Pinout (1200, 20-pin):
- 1: RES
- PD0
- PD1
- XTL2
- XTL1
- (INT0) PD2
- PD3
- (T0) PD4
- PD5
- GND (10)
- 11: PD6
- PB0(AIN0)
- PB1(AIN1)
- PB2
- PB3
- PB4
- PB5(MOSI)
- PB6(MISO)
- PB7(SCK)
- 20: VCC

- 89 Instructions
- 1k Bytes FLASH ROM
- 64 Bytes EEPROM
- 32 x 8 Registers
- 15 I/O ports
- VCC 2.7 - 6.0v
- Fully static 0 - 16MHz
- 8-bit timer/10-bit prescalar
- Watch Dog Timer
- Analogue Comparator

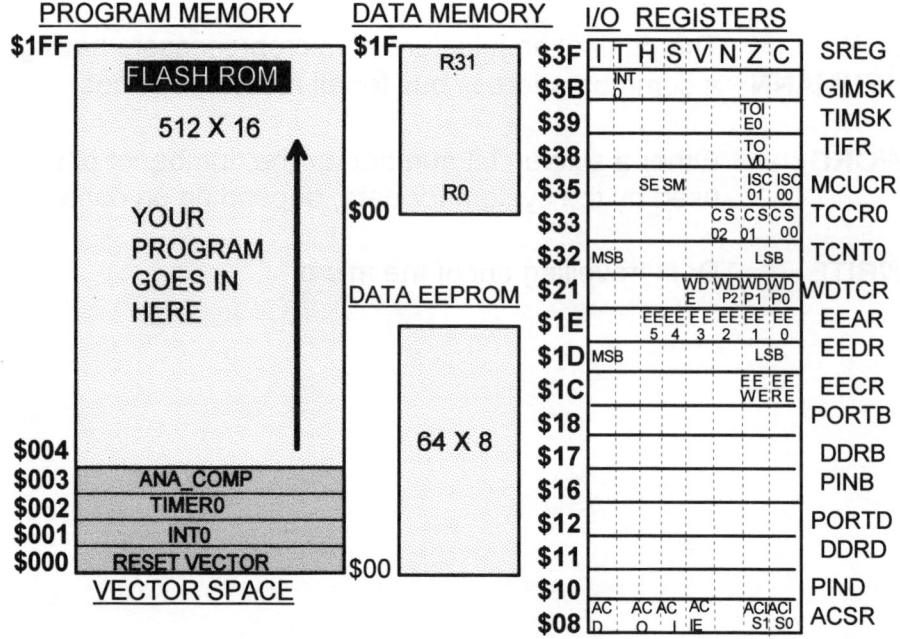

PROGRAM MEMORY

- $1FF — FLASH ROM, 512 X 16
- YOUR PROGRAM GOES IN HERE
- $004
- $003 ANA_COMP
- $002 TIMER0
- $001 INT0
- $000 RESET VECTOR
- VECTOR SPACE

DATA MEMORY

- $1F — R31
- $00 — R0
- DATA EEPROM: 64 X 8
- $00

I/O REGISTERS

Addr	Bits	Name
$3F	I T H S V N Z C	SREG
$3B	INT0	GIMSK
$39	TOIE0	TIMSK
$38	TOV0	TIFR
$35	SE SM ISC01 ISC00	MCUCR
$33	CS02 CS01 CS00	TCCR0
$32	MSB ... LSB	TCNT0
$21	WDE WDP2 WDP1 WDP0	WDTCR
$1E	EEAR5 EEAR4 EEAR3 EEAR2 EEAR1 EEAR0	EEAR
$1D	MSB ... LSB	EEDR
$1C	EEWE EERE	EECR
$18		PORTB
$17		DDRB
$16		PINB
$12		PORTD
$11		DDRD
$10		PIND
$08	ACD ACO ACIE ACI ACS1 ACS0	ACSR

APPENDIX B

INSTRUCTION SET KEYS

Status Register (SREG):

SREG: Status Register
C: Carry flag in status register
Z: Zero flag in status register
N: Negative flag in status register
V: Twos complement overflow indicator
S: N XOR V, for signed tests
H: Half Carry flag in the status register
T: Transfer bit used by BLD and BST instructions
I: Global interrupt enable/disable flag

Registers and Operands:

Rd: Destination (and source) register in the register file
Rr: Source register in the register file
R: Result after instruction is executed
K: Constant literal or byte data (8 bit)
k: Constant address data for program counter
b: Bit in the register file or I/O register (3 bit)
s: Bit in the status register (3 bit)

X,Y,Z: Indirect address register (X=R27:R26, Y=R29:R28 and Z=R31:R30)
P: I/O port address
q: Displacement for direct Addressing (6 bit)

APPENDIX B

AT90S1200 INSTRUCTION SET

Mnemonics	Operands	Description	Flags
ARITHMETIC AND LOGIC INSTRUCTIONS			
ADD	Rd, Rr	Add without Carry	Z,C,N,V,H
ADC	Rd, Rr	Add with Carry	Z,C,N,V,H
SUB	Rd, Rr	Subtract without Carry	Z,C,N,V,H
SUBI	Rd, K	Subtract Immediate	Z,C,N,V,H
SBC	Rd, Rr	Subtract with Carry	Z,C,N,V,H
SBCI	Rd, K	Subtract Immediate with Carry	Z,C,N,V,H
AND	Rd, Rr	Logical AND	Z,N,V
ANDI	Rd, K	Logical AND with Immediate	Z,N,V
OR	Rd, Rr	Logical OR	Z,N,V
ORI	Rd, K	Logical OR with Immediate	Z,N,V
EOR	Rd, Rr	Exclusive OR	Z,N,V
COM	Rd	One's Complement	Z,C,N,V
NEG	Rd	Two's Complement	Z,C,N,V,H
SBR	Rd, K	Set Bit(s) in Register	Z,N,V
CBR	Rd, K	Clear Bit(s) in Register	Z,N,V
INC	Rd	Increment	Z,N,V
DEC	Rd	Decrement	Z,N,V
TST	Rd	Test for Zero or Minus	Z,N,V
CLR	Rd	Clear Register	Z,N,V
SER	Rd	Set Register	None
CP	Rd, Rr	Compare	Z,C,N,V,H
CPC	Rd, Rr	Compare with Carry	Z,C,N,V,H
CPI	Rd, K	Compare with Immediate	Z,C,N,V,H
BRANCH INSTRUCTIONS			
RJMP	k	Relative Jump	None
RCALL	k	Relative Call Subroutine	None
RET		Subroutine Return	None
RETI		Interrupt Return	I
CPSE	Rd, Rr	Compare, Skip if Equal	None
SBRC	Rd, b	Skip if Bit in Register Cleared	None
SBRS	Rd, b	Skip if Bit in Register Set	None
SBIC	P, b	Skip if Bit in I/O Register Cleared	None
SBIS	P, b	Skip if Bit in I/O Register Set	None
BRBS	s, k	Branch if Status Flag Set	None
BRBC	s, k	Branch if Status Flag Cleared	None
BREQ	k	Branch if Equal	None
BRNE	k	Branch if Not Equal	None
BRCS	k	Branch if Carry Set	None
BRCC	k	Branch if Carry Cleared	None

APPENDIX B

BRSH	k	Branch if Same or Higher	None
BRLO	k	Branch if Lower	None
BRMI	k	Branch if Minus	None
BRPL	k	Branch if Plus	None
BRGE	k	Branch if Greater or Equal, Signed	None
BRLT	k	Branch if Less Than, Signed	None
BRHS	k	Branch if Half Carry Flag Set	None
BRHC	k	Branch if Half Carry Flag Cleared	None
BRTS	k	Branch if T Flag Set	None
BRTC	k	Branch if T Flag Cleared	None
BRVS	k	Branch if Overflow Flag Set	None
BRVC	k	Branch if Overflow Flag Cleared	None
BRIE	k	Branch if Interrupt Enabled	None
BRID	k	Branch if Interrupt Disabled	None
DATA TRANSFER INSTRUCTIONS			
MOV	Rd, Rr	Copy Register	None
LDI	Rd, K	Load Immediate	None
LD	Rd, Z	Load Indirect	None
ST	Z, Rd	Store Indiredt	None
IN	Rd, P	In Port	None
OUT	P, Rd	Out Port	None
BIT AND BIT-TEST INSTRUCTIONS			
LSL	Rd	Logical Shift Left	Z,C,N,V,H
LSR	Rd	Logical Shift Right	Z,C,N,V
ROL	Rd	Rotate Left Through Carry	Z,C,N,V,H
ROR	Rd	Rotate Right Through Carry	Z,C,N,V
ASR	Rd	Arithmetic Shift Right	Z,C,N,V
SWAP	Rd	Swap Nibbles	None
BSET	s	Flag Set	SREG(s)
BCLR	s	Flag Clear	SREG(s)
SBI	P, b	Set Bit in I/O Register	None
CBI	P, b	Clear Bit in I/O Register	None
BST	Rr, b	Bit Store from Register to T	T
BLD	Rd, b	Bit Load from T to Register	None
SEC		Set Carry	C
CLC		Clear Carry	C
SEN		Set Negative Flag	N
CLN		Clear Negative Flag	N
SEZ		Set Zero Flag	Z
CLZ		Clear Zero Flag	Z
SEI		Global Interrupt Enable	I
CLI		Global Interrupt Disable	I
SES		Set Signed Test Flag	S
CLS		Clear Signed Test Flag	S
SEV		Set Two's Complement Overflow Flag	V
CLV		Clear Two's Complement Overflow Flag	V

APPENDIX B

SET		Set T in SREG	T
CLT		Clear T in SREG	T
SEH		Set Half Carry Flag in SREG	H
CLH		Clear Half Carry Flag in SREG	H
NOP		No Operation	None
SLEEP		Sleep	None
WDR		Watchdog Reset	None

ADDITIONAL INSTRUCTIONS FOR OTHER AVR DEVICES

ARITHMETIC AND LOGIC INSTRUCTIONS			
ADIW	Rd, K	Add immediate to Word	Z, C, N, V
SBIW	Rd, K	Subtract Immediate from Word	Z, C, N, V
DATA TRANSFER INSTRUCTIONS			
LDS	Rd, k	Load Direct from SRAM	None
LD	Rd, X	Load Indirect	None
LD	Rd, X+	Load Indirect and Post-Increment	None
LD	Rd, -X	Load Indirect and Pre-Decrement	None
LD	Rd, Y	Load Indirect	None
LD	Rd, Y+	Load Indirect and Post-Increment	None
LD	Rd, -Y	Load Indirect and Pre-Decrement	None
LDD	Rd, Y+q	Load Indirect with Displacement	None
LD	Rd, Z	Load Indirect	None
LD	Rd, Z+	Load Indirect and Post-Increment	None
LD	Rd, -Z	Load Indirect and Pre-Decrement	None
LDD	Rd, Z+q	Load Indirect with Displacement	None
STS	k, Rr	Store Direct to SRAM	None
ST	X, Rr	Store Indirect	None
ST	X+, Rr	Store Indirect and Post-Increment	None
ST	-X, Rr	Store Indirect and Pre-Decrement	None
ST	Y, Rr	Store Indirect	None
ST	Y+, Rr	Store Indirect and Post-Increment	None
ST	Y-, Rr	Store Indirect and Pre-Decrement	None
STD	Y+q, Rr	Store Indirect with Displacement	None
ST	Z+, Rr	Store Indirect and Post-Increment	None
ST	-Z, Rr	Store Indirect and Pre-Decrement	None
STD	Z+q, Rr	Store Indirect with Displacement	None
LPM		Load Program Memory	None
PUSH	Rr	Push Register on Stack	None
POP	Rd	Pop Register from Stack	None

APPENDIX C

USEFUL REFERENCES

Atmel UK Sales Offices & Operations

Atmel U.K., Ltd.
Coliseum Business Centre
Riverside Way
Camberley, Surrey GU15 3YL
England
TEL (44) 1276-686677
FAX (44) 1276-686697

AVR Data

AVR SUPPORT PRODUCTS

AVR support products

EMBEDDED RESULTS LTD
PO BOX 200
ABERYSTWYTH
SY23 6WD
UK
PHONE / FAX +44 (0)8707 446 807

email:sales@kanda.com   www.kanda.com

AVR Starter Kit   -   Software, Programmer for
AT90S RANGE
In Circuit Emulator
Programming in C courses
5 day full board residential course in
conjunction with Chippenham College
using AVR MCUs and IAR
workbench.

INDEX

A

ADC	124
Addition	34
Addressing	
Modes	53
Analogue	7
AND	12
Assembler	90, 112, 121, 140

B

BCD	33
Binary	9, 31
Bit	11, 69
Byte	11, 69

C

C	4, 90, 138
Carry	61
CISC	4,
Clock	20, 42, 102
Code	83, 90, 97
CPU	18
Current	
Sink	43
Source	43

D

DAC	126
DEBUGGER	141
Decimal	30
Delay	102
Device	
Pinouts	40
Digital	7
Direct	54
DRAM	25

E

EEPROM	24, 37, 49, 51, 114
EOR	12, 14, 132
EPROM	3, 24, 37
Execute	19, 27

F

Fetch	18, 27
Firmware	93, 128, 134
FLASH	5, 24,
ROM	37, 45, 50

H

Hardware	88
Designs	92, 115, 124, 127
Harvard	19, 29
Hexadecimal	32

I

ICE	3, 37, 45, 133, 137
IIC	26
Immediate	62
Indirect	56
Input	65
Instruction	
set	53
Interrupt	39, 50, 72, 76, 130

L

LIBRARY	140
LINKER	140
Logic	
See AND,	
OR, EOR	

INDEX

M

MCU 47, 52, 73, 113
Memory 22
Microcontroller
  See mcu
MPU 7, 2, 37

N

Nibble 11
Noise 7, 10
NOT 15

O

Object 90
One's Complement 35
Operand 27
Operation
  Code 27
OR 12
OTP 3, 5
Output
  Ports 44, 66
Overflow 36

P

PIC 2, 37
PORT 44, 66
PWM 39, 122

R

RAM 22, 25
Register
  File 51
  I/O 52
Relative 58
Reset 41, 50
RISC 4
ROM 22, 37

S

Simulator 90
SLEEP
Source
  Code 97
SPI 26
SRAM 25, 48
Stack 70
Status 61
Subroutine 70
Subtraction 35

T

Table
  Look-up 114
Timer
  T0 79
  WDT 39, 48, 82 134
Truth Table 16
Two's
Complement 35

U

UART 26

V

Vector 49
Von Neuman 19, 27

W

Watchdog
  Timer 39, 48, 82, 134
WDT
  See Watchdog
Word 11

COMING SHORTLY

In-Circuit Emulators

- Kanda-ICE
- 51 ICEnse
- AVR ICEnce

PLD Starter Kit

Programmable Logic Devices (PLDs) provide the digital design engineer with an excellent flexibility and enhanced levels of security for any design. Costing less, in many cases, than the equivalent TTL they now come in enhanced flash versions that may be reprogrammed at will. This system takes the engineer from basic logic through the design process and up to the point where you can produce your own designs. The system includes everything you need to get started. Included are a full tutorial book, a training module, an enhanced copy of the Internationally acclaimed CUPL design language, a reprogrammable device (that can emulate a range of PALs) and an industrial strength programmer. All the design and programming functions are carried out through an integrated Windows desktop so producing a working design is a quick and painless task. The system is sold for less than the cost of a programmer on its own.

System includes:

- Integrated Design Environment with automated template generator.
- Training book with application examples and step by step tutorials
- Free copy of the Industry Standard CUPL
- Small footprint programmer
- Flash based, reprogrammable device
- PC Connection lead
- Hard wearing carrying case

AVR Starter Kit 40-pin Adapter

This adapter can be used with the AVR Starter Kit to programme 40 Pin devices. The following devices can be programmed :

- Atmel AT90S8515
- Atmel AT89S8252
- Atmel AT89S54

Serial EEPROM Starter Kit

This starter Kit includes everything you need to programme the following EEPROMS :

- Atmel AT25XXX series (SPI)
- Atmel AT24CXX series (2-wire)
- Atmel AT93CXX series (3-wire)
- Atmel AT56CXX series (4-wire)
- Atmel AT17CXX series FPGA configuration memories

The Kit contains :

- Kanda Systems Windows programming software with FREE upgrades.
- Programming Module(battery operated for portability).
- Programming cable and dongle.
- Full Technical Support.
- In-system programming via an IDC connector.

Other Products From KANDA Systems

AVR Starter Kit

The AVR starter kit includes everything you need to realise your Flash AVR microcontroller designs. The package comprises :
- In-System Programming cable and dongle
- Programming Module (battery operated so very portable).
- Assemblers - Atmel & IAR
- Software Simulator
- Kanda AVR ISP for Windows Software to programme your devices.
- EMC compatible IDC layout
- Packaged in rugged case.

Write your code - assemble - simulate - programme in system.

Universal Programmer

The NEW Universal Programmer can now program the following devices.
- Most 8051 derivative microcontroller e.g Atmel
- The AVR RISC Microcontroller from Atmel
- EPROM's
- Serial and Parallel EEPROMs

The package includes instruction manual, Window based software, is battery powered, FREE software updates and comprehensive technical support.

Other Titles coming shortly

Get going with ..... FPGAs

This is the second book in the series of 'fast track' books to help you learn about and design with new technology. This book takes you from basic logic principles to in-depth design examples based on the latest Atmel FPGA offering - the 40K

Get going with ..... IAR 'C' for Microcontrollers.

Ever wanted to learn 'C' easily and quickly? This could be the ideal medium for you. This book is written by an embedded microcontroller specialist for embedded microcontroller designs. It goes from design basics to real 'C' code examples.

Get going with ..... PLD's

From basic logic design, through basic PLD exercises to more in-depth useful design examples. Included in this package is enhanced CUPL - a design description language and design simulator. Also an enhancement to the software courtesy of Kanda Systems for design template generation.

Fax Back Form

Name

Company

Address

Country   Postcode

I would like

more information on other products .   ☐

to be included on your mailing list for future products   ☐

Fax No : (+44)(+0) 1970 621040

Tel No : (+44) (+0) 1970 621030

Web Site : http://www.kanda-systems.com